The Grand Challenge

From the 20th to the 21st Century: Transcending the Faultline

The Grand Challenge

From the 20th to the 21st Century : Transcending the Faultline

Keiko Takahashi

Sampoh Publishing Co., Ltd.

Tokyo

The Grand Challenge
Keiko Takahashi

Translated by Duncan Ryuken Williams

Published by Sampoh Publishing Co., Ltd., 1-17-4 Azumabashi, Sumida-ku, Tokyo, 130-0001.
Originally published in Japanese under the title "Gurando Charenji" by Sampoh Publishing
Co., Ltd., Tokyo, copyright ©1998 by Keiko Takahashi. English translation copyright
©2002 by Keiko Takahashi. All rights reserved. Printed in Japan.
First edition, 2002

ISBN4-87928-039-9

CONTENTS

CHAPTER 4
The Inception of the Grand Challenge (To Look within Ourselves)

CHAPTER 5

The Inception of the Grand Challenge (To Connect Our Inner Selves and the Outer World)

INTRODUCTION

The Declaration of the Grand Challenge

This is a story told by a certain European who lived in China. There was a time long ago when a certain region of China was hit by a severe drought. No matter how much people prayed, there was no rain. The situation got worse and worse and the villagers decided to ask a sage who could make rain for help. A sage was brought in from the next region over, and when he got to the village he asked for a small, quiet lodge. He then sequestered himself in the lodge.

On the fourth day, clouds began gathering in the sky and though it wasn't winter, out of that sky came a huge snowstorm. All everyone could talk about was the rain-making sage. The European visitor, who witnessed this event, went to see the sage. He asked him, "How did you make it snow?" The old man replied, "I didn't make it snow. It had nothing to do with me." "Then, what were you doing for those three days?" asked the European.

"That's simple enough," replied the old man. "I had just come from a region where everything was in order and all was balanced because people lived in accord with Heaven. However, this village was in a state of disarray when I arrived, so I had to spend time in the lodge until I could return to the Tao (the Way) so that rain would fall naturally."

(Adapted from C.G. Jung, *Collected Works*, Vol. 14)

Spiritual Deepening in the New Age

The 21st century is to come upon us. The third millennium. What kind of reality will we face in this new age? We do not yet know the shape of this new era. The upcoming thousand years awaits us as an unknown future.

But what we are certain of is that the new age will involve the beginning of a new stage in human "spiritual deepening." This is a critical task in the midst of myriad problems and limitations faced by humankind today. I would like to, first of all, direct our attention to the challenges that lie ahead to accomplish this new "spiritual deepening."

So what is the new human "spiritual deepening"? The human being is the only creature that ties together both the "spiritual world" and the "phenomenal world." What I mean by the "spiritual world" is the vast and unlimited inner world, an invisible spiritual world. The "phenomenal world" is the visible world around us, which also expands infinitely. These two unbounded dimensions are simultaneously embodied by the human being. The new age of human "spiritual deepening" will need to involve human beings truly living out their humanness, that is, to attend to both the spiritual and phenomenal worlds.

Humans, as the steward of all creatures, have been vested with the ability to tie the spiritual and phenomenal worlds together. With this authority, humans have powers which other creatures don't have. For example, the ability to "solve things." This function is related to the process of internalizing various kinds of problems from the outer, phenomenal world. This internal process further involves finding a key (solution) that will fit a keyhole (problem) and thus "solve things" by opening a new door.

In the case of medicine, for example, the discovery of new cures and medicines occurs because medical doctors and researchers internalize "the pain" that exists in the outer world. This internalization process involves the discovery of a key (new cures and medicines) that can treat or cure ailments (the keyhole) that pervade the world.

To take another example, how about human "creativity"? To create something involves taking an intention, a hope, or a vision from the inner world and actualizing it into a given form in the outer world. For example, countless people in human history have wanted to fly like birds in the sky. And in the nineteenth century, many different kinds of flying machines and airplanes were designed and tried out. But for nearly 100 years, the barrier of a 100-meter flight was not broken until the Wright brothers' airplane. Their plane came into being because they chose, from the limitless possibilities in the conditions of the outer world, the best combination for flying the plane. These included the plane's wing (its shape, number, width, length), the atmosphere (the air density and viscosity), and the relationship between gravity and lift. The important point here is that they actualized their creativity and inner vision by following the blueprint for the plane that existed within their minds.

Although all human activity necessarily involves this type of inter-action between the inner and outer worlds, unfortunately, we human beings have not been able to fully embody this connection between the two worlds. Indeed, while the embodiment of the spiritual and phe-nomenal worlds is a human birthright, no one has been able to truly achieve its connection. However, the embodiment of the two worlds is precisely the key that will open the door to the spiritual deepening and evolution of human beings. This is the calling of our age. This evolu-tion is akin to the evolutionary shift that creatures made when they emerged from the sea to become land-based creatures. This spiritual deepening is an opportunity for us human beings that has never been presented to us before.

The Limitations of the 20th Century, Which Separated the Inner Self and the Outer World

Throughout history, whenever humans have faced a crisis or reached some kind of limit, to overcome these obstacles, they have inevitably looked to the outer world to clear out a new avenue. Without excep-tion, the great civilizations (for example, the empires of Alexander the Great, the Roman Empire, or the Mongol Empire of Ghengis Khan) all tried to expand their territory further and further out to open up new possibilities. The movement of European nations after the six-teenth century went beyond the conflicts among the nations them-selves, to an assertion of their national strength through colonial expansion to the new, unexplored continents such as Africa and the New World of the Americas.

And with the explosive growth of science, in the 20th century, humans advanced into space, which was formerly a realm of awe and mystery. This reflects the same obsession with exploring the outer lim-its of the world. Using massive resources (both economic and human) to marshal the best in science, humans were able to launch space rockets and unmanned satellites. This reflects one extreme form of the 20th-century choice of "outward expansion." Another example might be the extracting of resources from the outer world, such as iron or oil, to fuel this quest.

Taking the inner world lightly, we humans have focused exclusively on the possibilities in the outer, phenomenal world. And especially in the 20th century, this has led to the separation between the inner and outer, the spiritual and phenomenal, worlds. The result of this separation, however, is the current, problem-filled world in which we live.

These problems include the current economic situation in which the prolonged recession and the depressed stock market caused by financial deregulation have caused instability in Japan. The currency worries in Asia, the banking scandals, and the corruption at the Finance Ministry have all come together to shake the Japanese economic system at its roots.

Problems also include the explosion in juvenile crimes in which minors suddenly break out in rage because of all the uncertainty. Further, environmental pollution issues such as hormone disrupters which not only affect the environment generally, but behave in our bodies like hormones and affect reproductive function, threatening the very existence of the human species.

Surely, these are all ways in which the world is telling us "No" to the way we have lived our lives. Optimistically prolonging it is not an option. Reality is making perfectly clear to us that we can no longer separate the spiritual and phenomenal worlds.

The Declaration of the Grand Challenge : To Look within Ourselves and to Connect Our Inner Selves and the Outer World

Though the spiritual and phenomenal worlds have not met in the past, when these two dimensions are truly integrated, there is a moment in which the two unbounded realms resonate. The power that emerges in that moment is one akin to the explosive energy produced when matter and anti-matter come together, creating a hitherto unimaginable power.

What we human beings require in the present day is, put simply:

to look within ourselves (mind) and **to connect our inner selves** (mind) **and the outer world** (reality).

If we are able to live in this way, it would be as if an arid desert is transformed into a green and vibrant forest. It would reverberate around the world and even resonate with the way of the universe itself. This way of living would be able to respond to the **universal principle of integration**, turn darkness into light, and transform disorder into a new life of harmony.

This process is similar to the call by the leading religious figures in history, all of whom encourage us to find a path that delivers us from the fundamental karmic conditions of human beings (the karma of biology, environment, and the age). These religious greats all spent their lives looking within themselves and connecting their inner selves and the outer world. First of all, they all looked into their inner selves with great attention. Based on such an investigation of the self, they opened themselves up to the sufferings and sins of others and without qualms took on these sufferings and sins as their own. Taking on the karmic conditions from the outer world, they drew in the pain of others. Precisely because of that, they were able to discover a path to free people so that they might embark on their mission in life.

This process, **to look within ourselves** and **to connect our inner selves and the outer world** is what will bring about the new age of the 21st century. This is the **Grand Challenge** itself! The **Grand Challenge** is not simply some newfangled technique for living, but a fundamental shift in the very assumptions on the way we ought to live as well as the way in which the human and the world ought to interact. It is a new challenge to return to the original nature of human beings, that is, the integration of the spiritual and phenomenal worlds. This is "The Declaration of the **Grand Challenge**," an entry point to a new way of living, to which we will be referring throughout this book.

In the story of the rain-making sage at the beginning of this book, we saw how instead of tackling the external reality of the drought, he first attended to his internal reality. Instead of cutting off his inner reality from the external reality, he adjusted his internal mindset to the Tao (the Way) of the universe. This led to the miraculous result of rain falling in a land of drought, a miracle sent from Heaven.

About 700 years ago, when the Japanese faced unprecedented

threats from Mongol invaders, who had inspired fear with their expansion throughout the Eurasian plateau, Japan's leader, Hojo Tokimune (1251-84) faced this situation in a similar manner. Tokimune visited Mugaku Sogen (1226-86), his Zen master, to report the imminent invasion of the Mongols. He was told to remain clear-minded so as not to get caught up in delusions about their power, but to see them for what they were. This advice proved to be essential for Tokimune, who prayed fervently for half a year, but simultaneously figured out concrete ways to repel the vastly more powerful Mongol invaders, such as assembling his troops in the probable site of the invasion, the Kyushu Island, and erecting stone fortifications. In doing all he could with his clear mind and leaving the rest up to fate, Japan was able to escape this crisis when "heavenly winds" (kamikaze) sunk the Mongol ships.

This episode reflects the process of the **Grand Challenge** which transcends history. Mugaku Sogen accepted the external crisis into himself while Tokimune, upon hearing his master's advice, acted by inner prayer and outer concrete actions. In both men, they chose not to separate their inner selves and the outer world. Surely, when people prepare themselves like this, miracles can happen.

The **Grand Challenge** represents what can happen when one goes beyond human will to align oneself with the will of the universe itself. This is the path created when the infinite universes of the inner and outer worlds come into full integration.

The Theory and Practice of the Grand Challenge

This book is divided into five chapters according to the Buddhist concept of **Causes of Suffering (Present Situation-Causes)-Elimination of the Causes of Suffering (Enlightenment)-the Path**.

Chapter 1 : The Path of Resonating with the Universe — This chapter takes up the main questions and themes of the Grand Challenge. The purpose of looking deeply within will be contextualized within the framework of resonating with the universe.

Chapter 2 : A New Paradigm to Understand the Inner and Outer Worlds — Two pillars to actualize the Grand Challenge are taken up in this chapter.

Chapter 3: The Soul Compass — This chapter provides a series of coordinates for looking within ourselves and connecting our inner selves and the outer world. We are invited to look deeply and precisely at the true nature of the various problems we might shoulder.

Chapter 4: The Inception of the Grand Challenge (To Look within Ourselves) — A guide to the practice of the Grand Challenge. We are invited to reflect concretely on the process of looking within ourselves by using, among other tools, the **Reflections and Insight Sheet**.

Chapter 5: The Inception of the Grand Challenge (To Connect Our Inner Selves and the Outer World) — A further guide to the path of turning a dark, negative reality into a positive, light-filled reality by using the practice of **In-En-Kahoh**. There are also hints on the wisdom of how to embody the practice.

After each chapter, there is a section "A Record of an Individual's Grand Challenge." Since many people have already tried to implement the **Grand Challenge** in their lives, these records serve as a testament to their practice. By reading these records, we can see the types of things people realized on the Grand Challenge path and learn how to clearly see our own futures from them.

The **Grand Challenge** is a challenge that anyone can undertake. Though it is critical calling of our times, we must not forget that as human beings, it is also a timeless challenge that requires a measure of courage. It is a path open to anyone, a path of miraculous awakening and transformation, which comes about step by step, leading to a new page in human history.

It is my sincere wish that the reader might take on this **Grand Challenge** in a way that comes close to the reality of each individual reader. Walking this path, step by step, I hope each reader might envision a new world and create a new reality.

	Structure		Keywords
Chapter 1 The Path of Resonating with the Universe	The State of Enlightenment That Pervades All Things (The Underlying Theme)		Six Forces
Chapter 2 A New Paradigm to Understand the Inner and Outer Worlds	The State of Enlightenment (Ultimate Purpose)	The 21st Century The Other Side of the Faultline	Chaos Mind-and-Form Unit
Chapter 3 The Soul Compass	Causes of Suffering (Present Situation-Causes)	The 20th Century This Side of the Faultline	Four Blades
Chapter 4 The Inception of the Grand Challenge (To Look within Ourselves)	The Path (Method-Means)	From the 20th to the 21st Century (Transcending the Faultline)	To Look within Ourselves
Chapter 5 The Inception of the Grand Challenge (To Connect Our Inner Selves and the Outer World)			To Connect Our Inner Selves and the Outer World

Chart 0 : The Overall Structure as Described in This Book

CHAPTER 1

The Path of Resonating with the Universe

	Structure		Keywords
Chapter 1 The Path of Resonating with the Universe	The State of Enlightenment That Pervades All Things （The Underlying Theme）		Six Forces
Chapter 2 A New Paradigm to Understand the Inner and Outer Worlds	The State of Enlightenment （Ultimate Purpose）	The 21st Century The Other Side of the Faultline	Chaos Mind-and-Form Unit
Chapter 3 The Soul Compass	Causes of Suffering （Present Situation-Causes）	The 20th Century This Side of the Faultline	Four Blades
Chapter 4 The Inception of the Grand Challenge （To Look within Ourselves）	The Path （Method-Means）	From the 20th to the 21st Century （Transcending the Faultline）	To Look within Ourselves
Chapter 5 The Inception of the Grand Challenge （To Connect Our Inner Selves and the Outer World）			To Connect Our Inner Selves and the Outer World

From the 20th to the 21st Century : Transcending the Faultline

The Paradox of Civilization

As we stand on the precipice of a new millennium and begin the **Grand Challenge**, the divide between the 20th century (where we stand at present) and the upcoming 21st century (which is in view in the horizon) is vast.

Humankind has been able to rise to many different kinds of challenges during the 20th century through new philosophies and scientific innovations. But in the process of making gains, is it not the case that we have also lost many valuable things as well? While solving problems in various fields, at the same time, problems inconceivable prior to the 20th century were also born.

In other words, the creation of solutions also involved the creation of problems. What was at one time a great beacon of civilization often became a stranglehold on humanity. Human civilization, thus, has precipitated this paradox. If we continue on our current model of civilization, we will not only be unable to solve the problems of the present, but we will be unable to cross over the faultline into the future.

The Growing Complexity, Enormity, and Rapid Rise of Problems

The problems we currently face are different, both in their enormity and in their nature, from the problems humankind has ever faced before. Three aspects—**complexity**, **enormity**, and **rapid rise**—characterize our current situation.

What I mean by **complexity** is that any given problem is interconnected to a complex of other problems. For example, with the problem of bullying, there has been, in recent years in Japan, a rise in cases of bullying where meanness has led to hurt and even suicide. However, it is impossible to isolate "the problem of bullying" from other issues. The situation is hard to assess, in part, because of the complex factors that go into creating this problem. They include problems within the educational system, the family and the children themselves, or with teacher training and even with society at large which looms as the backdrop to all of these problems. The problem of environmental pollution is also similar in that one would need to look at the interconnections between the problems inherent in science and technology, economics, the population explosion, and everyday life style in contemporary society.

Further, the problems we face today are on a scale incomparable to earlier times. The **enormity** of our problems is certainly reflected in the global nature of environmental issues, for example. Problems facing the environment transcend boundaries, affecting global economics and life style, in such a way as to preclude a piecemeal approach to solving them. Another aspect of the enormity of our current situation is the ability that humans have developed in the 20th century to destroy not only themselves, but the entire earth, multiple times over with nuclear weapons. Thus, compared with the destructive capability of just 100 years ago, we humans have developed a capacity to cause problems on a massive scale.

The **rapid rise** of problems, especially in the way in which one problem can quickly affect other areas, is also a cause for concern. For example, in the arena of economics, when information about an economy or fiscal policy can be transmitted in an instant across the world, markets react swiftly to this news. With the yen-dollar exchange rate, for example, its daily fluctuations cause serious concern for industries whose very existence might be put in question by the up- and downtick of one yen. These rapid changes in industries can, then, further affect national economies as well.

The Grand Challenge Which Crosses over the Faultline to the 21st Century

What is important to note here is that the complexity, enormity, and rapid rise of problems we currently face is a sign from the world that the course humankind has elected is not the correct one. The world is telling us "No." These problems constitute a great barrier that divides us from the new world and age, a barrier which seemingly presents us with a never-ending slew of problems.

This barrier can only be overcome if we let go of the 20th-century ways of problem-solving and shift to a completely new 21st-century paradigm, a new set of principles that will enable us undertake the **Grand Challenge**. As the first step, we ought to examine the premises of our challenge. What is "Grand" about the **Grand Challenge**? What, exactly, is the **Grand Challenge**?

The Century of Self-Aggrandizement

We are at a point in history when we can look back retrospectively unto the 20th century as a whole. While there is always a danger of oversimplification, can it not be said that the 20th century was a century of human self-aggrandizement?

For example, the 20th century made great strides in science. It is certainly a wonder that gradually we have unlocked the secrets of the natural world. However, this constant attempt to scientifically analyze nature hides an unbounded greed. This is because the very existence of things unknown threatens the "self" which is sustained by knowledge and control over all things. By obtaining a commanding knowledge of all of nature's secrets, humans have attempted to aggrandize their self over nature.

Humans have also made great advances in tackling sufferings of all kinds. Throughout history, three causes of suffering (poverty, illness, and war) have provided constant problems for human beings. For most of history, these three conditions were feared as a continual reminder of nature's prerogative over human will. Although we must be aware of pockets of suffering that still exist, the overall trend has been a historical movement toward the gradual elimination of these forms of suffering, suggesting a parallel trend of human dominance over the world.

In the arena of medicine, treatments and cures emerged for a huge range of diseases and illnesses. The structure of a human life, bestowed to us in this world—birth, old age, illness, and death—includes aging, illnesses and death that are incumbent to the process. But the advances in medicine have attempted to resist the very structures of a human life course. In the area of poverty, too, especially in advanced industrial nations, economic production has reached such a level of prosperity that is incomparable to any period in the past. Just in the past 30 years, the Japanese GNP has increased fifteen times. With war, Japan has been conflict-free for over a half century.

In this model of ever-increasing prosperity, human arrogance has developed to the point where it has tried to become utterly dominant over the world, squeezing out all of nature's resources for its only selfish greed. In other words, while at one point in human history, the world overwhelmed the human, we have come to the point when humans have accumulated enough capabilities to overwhelm the world.

Toward a Millennium of Resonance with the Universe

Humans were supposed to have dominated the world, brought all of nature to its knees, and through such control have achieved unprecedented contentment according to the narrative of ever-increasing prosperity. But this expectation has been collapsing all around us in the late 20th century. Human self-aggrandizement not only produced positive results, but brought with it a myriad of dark, negative consequences as well.

When humans tried to develop in this self-aggrandizing manner, we attempted to seek out ways to become independent from the world around us. Although such "independence" has its positive points and must be seen as an important stage in human development, such a stance cannot help us over the barrier that we face today, made of both positive and negative conditions. A new stage in human history must involve "giving up the self" to the world and learning how to live in **resonance with the world**. This means going beyond gain or loss for an individual self, so as to look to the good of others or the whole world, in other words, living not in an antagonistic way toward the world, but in a harmonious manner.

To live in resonance with the world means that we no longer try to squeeze out gain from one another and the world, but to promote a pluralistic community of beings that respects individuals that live, resonate, and work together in harmony. Rather than take from the world, we must give back to it so that a new world might be created. If self-aggrandizement was the impulse of the 20th century, the 21st century must be characterized by the new outlook of **resonance with the world and universe** that will enable us to cross the great divide between the present and the future.

The Six Forces

The World Filled with the Six Forces

Resonance with the world and universe starts with recovering a sense of awe about the world around us: nature, the earth, and the universe. We cannot cut ourselves off from the universe; our existence depends completely on it. We are but a part of the great universe.

The "place" on which we live, the planet earth, emerges from the expansion of the cosmos of billions of light years. The "now" that we live in is but a moment in the flow of billions of years of cosmic history. Although it may be quite impossible to imagine the extent of the vast universe, the same matter that makes up the universe is what makes us up, what flows through the universe flows through us.

The atoms, molecules, and biological cell structures that make up the planets, stars, and galaxies, also make us up. We share the same history, memory, and forces as such structures from the beginnings of the universe. In other words, there is a force that is the basis of all life, its evolution, as well as all the events in human history and civilization. This force pervades the entire world and without a sound grasp of this force, we are unable to resonate with the world nor incorporate any forces to accomplish things.

This force that pervades the world is the source we need to look to cross the faultline between us and the 21st century. Although this force is simultaneously infinitely large and small and while its nature as such is beyond human comprehension, it is possible to understand its appearance in six ways. I have called these the "**six forces**."

The **six forces** are: 1) **flow**, 2) **circulation**, 3) **linkage**, 4) **structure**, 5) **balance**, and 6) **eruption** (see Chart 1).

The Force to Move the Metasystemic World

Our world is a living entity which has been able to maintain equilibrium over an infinite period of time. It has kept this harmony continuously, despite including within itself all types of life forms. While this fact is not something we ponder on a daily basis, if we think about it, it is truly a miracle that this world continues to exist in the way it does. Our world is truly a multi-dimensional world.

This is evidenced by looking at both the macro- and microcosmic aspects of our world. In macrocosmic terms, the world is made up of the earth, the solar system, and galaxies. In microcosmic terms, the world is constituted of the biological matter that makes up our bodies, in other words, fundamental units of life such as molecules, atoms, and elementary particles. In this multi-dimensional world, all beings including animals, plants, and minerals are able to coexist in a vital way.

How does this world, which is such a complex meta-system, continue to exist from time immemorial? The answer lies in the true nature of the **six forces** we discussed above. Although the 20th century saw the emergence of many different inventions and systems, all things that have depended on human ingenuity are fragile. Human systems that last 100 years are rare, while those that last 1,000 years can almost be considered a miracle. Although the 20th century was able to create a high-level of material civilization through the use of capital resources and new technologies, the power that went into this civilization utilized only a minute segment of the **six forces**. The **six forces** are in fact a massive resource existing beyond both capital and technology.

The Six Forces (in Detail)

The **six forces** lie at the foundations of all existence, ensuring their creation, growth, and demise. From time immemorial in the past to the future, from the largest macrocosm to the smallest microcosm, there is not a thing in the universe that exists outside the **six forces**. Let us explore each of the **six forces** in more detail.

FLOW

Flow is the force that moves and changes things. All things and beings in the world, without exception, are in constant flux, never able to permanently remain the same. In Buddhism, this is described as "All is impermanent."

As one grows old, one's body weakens. To live necessarily means that one day one will die. There is not a single person that can escape this process of birth-old age-illness-and-death. The force of flow is this principle of flux.

The law of entropy, the theory that all things disintegrate in the physical world, also reflects the force of flow. Physical properties such as tobacco smoke rising and permeating the air or the inability to separate out hot and cold water once they've been mixed can also be explained by this principle.

CIRCULATION

Circulation is the force that moves things in a circular fashion. While the force of **flow** is unidirectional, the force of circulation moves things in a circular motion back to the beginning. For example, if we think about water circulation in living systems, water can take multiple forms. Water can be a liquid, but it also has a solid and gaseous form changing into clouds, rain, rivers, or the sea. At times this multi-dimensional water takes liquid form in our human bodies. However varied its form, the nature of water as H_2O never changes and the total amount of water never increases nor decreases. The force of circulation sustains our lives not only in the case of water, but in processes such as the circulation of blood and other bodily fluids within our bodies which enables organs and other tissue to exist by providing oxygen and nutrients.

LINKAGE

Linkage is the force that connects. All things in this world exist inter-connected with other things. There is nothing that exists autono-mously. Our bodies as well as our minds are intimately connected to external events and relationships. We are not isolated, but connected to the whole.

All material things are composed of molecules, which are in turn, composed of multiple atoms. In the case of water (H_2O), two hydro-gen atoms come into a relationship with one oxygen atom. The impulse to have a stable, rather than an unstable, combination is also related to the force of linkage. While there are a great number of dif-ferent phenomena, they are all composed of variations and combina-tions of atom sets as above. In Buddhism, this is described as "All things are without self" or the idea that things don't have an autonomous "self," which in turn, suggests the notion that every indi-vidual thing is connected to the whole.

STRUCTURE

Structure is the force that provides frameworks to things. Although the forces of **flow** and **linkage** allow things to exist in numerous, ever-changing combinations, this does not mean that things exist in dis-array. Rather, there is an impulse toward self-defining combinations which are structured in certain ways.

For example, if we examine our internal organs, they are made up of cells. These cells naturally die off, but new cells replace the old so that the organ can function normally. With the epithelial cells of the stomach, for instance, it is said that new cells replace the old every two to three days. Our bodies are thus always in flux and the organs only exist in relation to other organs. While organs thus **flow** and have **linkage** with one another, they don't just haphazardly exist, but they function by maintaining a **structure** of their own. The structures exist at multiple levels. The structure not only exists in the various organs (heart, lungs, liver, or kidneys), but at the sublevels of tissues, cells, molecules, and atoms. Thus the world exists by being structured on multiple levels.

BALANCE

Balance is the force that produces equilibrium. However complex and multi-dimensional the world, it never loses the quality of balance and equilibrium. Whether it's the circulation of water or the organs in a human body, their constant flux simultaneously entails balance.

Looking at the cosmos, the fact that numerous galaxies, stars, planets as well as life itself can coexist is based on a delicate balance fundamental to the universe. Although the universe is said to be constantly expanding (the Big Bang theory), the fact that stars can maintain constant formations is because the gravitational force between stars and the expansionary force of the universe as a whole are wonderfully balanced. If it weren't balanced and the expansionary force of the universe was stronger than the gravitational force between stars, the stars would be unable to exist. Likewise, if the gravitational force between stars were any stronger, stars would be pulled together to devastating effect. This kind of equilibrium is found in the tiniest elementary particles of the universe as well.

ERUPTION

Eruption is the force that gives new life. The world is not simply maintained by the five forces described above, but the force of **eruption** constantly gives new life to the universe. For example, the sun gives out tremendous heat and light into space, plants generate oxygen, while human bodies while alive continually create new cells. This vital energy and force gives life to the universe. That is to say, the universe is not

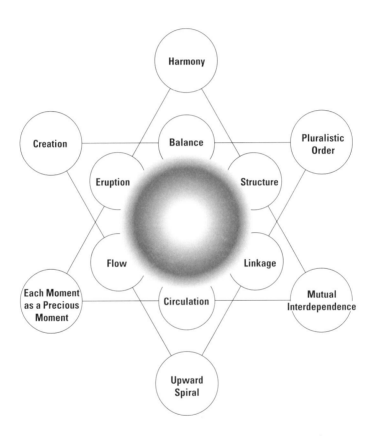

Chart 1 : The Six Forces

simply maintained in a static formation, but is a vital entity which continually brings forth new events and phenomena.

The Light and Darkness of the Six Forces

Up to now, we have explored the **six forces** as they exist in the natural and cosmic worlds. However, because the **six forces** pervade all phenomena in the universe, by extension, they equally exist in human society, national life, or an individual's inner world. What we must emphasize here, however, is that the **six forces** have both light and dark sides to them.

Human history can be understood as an interplay of light and darkness. For when there has been freedom, there have also been restrictions. With riches, there has been poverty, with liberation, oppression. In other words, while beacons of light have existed in human history, they have also been accompanied by the darkness of genocide, destruction, and self-conceit. The two extremes of light and darkness. These have also been created by the **six forces**. The **six forces** stand out especially when human society has undergone a major transformation and evolution.

When society faces a seemingly insurmountable barrier, the **six forces** enable society to clear those hurdles. The light provided by the **six forces** (the **six positive conditions**) at times appears in the form of people rising up to a challenge, a philosophy which draws people to a better society, or a new Zeitgeist (spirit of the times) that propels the world forward.

In contrast, societies have also seen the dark side of the **six forces** (the **six negative conditions**). The same **six forces** can, on other occasions, create unbelievably horrid conditions sparked in war, philosophies which encourage the use of violence, or the sudden disintegration of a high civilization.

Thus the **six forces** can propel both light and darkness in human society as seen in the following chart (Chart 2).

Flow : Each Moment as a Precious Moment or Instant Gratification

If the force of **flow** is positively channeled, it leads us to the experience of **each moment as a precious moment**, which is the notion that each moment is unique unto itself. Each stagnant condition can be trans-

Darkness			Light	
The Law of Disintegration			**The Universal Principle of Integration**	
INSTANT GRATIFICATION	Instant gratification in a world falling apart	**FLOW**	To take each moment as a precious moment given to us by the universe	**EACH MOMENT AS A PRECIOUS MOMENT**
DOWNWARD SPIRAL	Negative conditions keep repeating in a vicious cycle	**CIRCULATION**	Moving into a positive direction in a way that builds on each other	**UPWARD SPIRAL**
ENCROACHMENT ON OTHERS	A negative influence spreads throughout the web of life	**LINKAGE**	The part and whole mutually depend on each other to live in harmony	**MUTUAL INTERDEPENDENCE**
CONFORMITY	The self is subsumed into a conformist framework	**STRUCTURE**	A pluralistic vision of the world in which each individual is honored as part of the whole	**PLURALISTIC ORDER**
STAGNATION	The six forces and the system as a whole stand still	**BALANCE**	All things are in their proper place, which leads to stability	**HARMONY**
DESTRUCTION	Going against the true way of the world lays the seeds of destruction	**ERUPTION**	New creations are born continuously	**CREATION**
SIX NEGATIVE CONDITIONS		SIX FORCES		SIX POSITIVE CONDITIONS

Chart 2 : The Light and Darkness of the Six Forces

formed into a new positive direction. For instance, in the Japanese tradition of tea ceremony, there is the attitude that every occasion of extending hospitality at tea to another person might be the last time that such an occasion might come about. In other words, one should make the occasion a perfect and memorable one because it might not happen again. This orientation toward treating **each moment as a precious moment** is the positive way in which the **flow** can be understood.

However, the **flow**, because of its transient or momentary nature, can also be channeled into a negative direction. Each moment, viewed as the last moment, can also lead to an ethos of **instant gratification**. Because the world is thought of as haphazard and unpredictable, one can be led to live only for the moment. In other words, instead of living *in the moment* (**each moment as a precious moment**), a negative orientation would be to live *for the moment* (**instant gratification**).

Circulation : Upward Spiral or Downward Spiral

The force of **circulation** can also be understood as having both positive and negative impulses. On the one hand, the momentum of **circulation** can create an **upward spiral** in which the world is not simply flowing in a circle, but evolving in a positive direction. This is a spiral that is beyond life and death, increase or decrease. For example, the evolution of the many species on this planet has depended on this force of **circulation** to develop over several billion years.

On the other hand, circulation can also be transformed into a **downward spiral** in which one repeatedly falls into a vicious cycle of unending negative consequences. The pollution of the natural world, which leads to ongoing negative consequences for the ecosystem, is an example of this.

This type of circulation works not only in the natural world, but in human relations as well. Whether it be in the family, at work, or on an individual-to-individual basis, if trust and communications work in a healthy and positive manner, not only are everyday encounters positive, but even when problems arise, this positive energy propels an **upward spiral** that can overcome problems. However, if there is a lack of communication or good will, even ordinary situations can degenerate into a negative pattern in which new problems occur as we fall into a rut.

Linkage : Mutual Interdependence or Encroachment on Others

The force of **linkage** causes us to realize that we live in **mutual interdependence** on each other in an open system. When we see these links, we take the positive step of seeing the welfare and benefit of others as our own welfare and benefit. However, because we are all connected, when a negative phenomenon occurs, it can't be contained as it encroaches on all the other beings in the web of life. This **linkage** in its negative mode consists of **encroachment on others**.

Because the part is connected to the whole, when the 1997 Thai currency crisis erupted, the financial impact spread quickly to Hong Kong and Korea and even Japan and eventually led to currency and economic downturns of South East Asia. At present, the world's eyes are on Japan because it is clear that if Japan's financial industries collapse, it would spark a global crisis, putting into question Japan's responsibility not only to itself but to the world. However, if each nation brought about an economic restructuring of the type that reflected sound economic policies, the **mutual interdependence** of economics in an ever-increasing global and open system would bring about prosperity for all.

Structure : Pluralistic Order or Conformity

The force of **structure** is one that gives order to the world. When this **structure** is moved positively, it allows for a **pluralistic order** in which individual people and things coexist in a tolerant environment. In such a world, each individual reflects the whole and the whole reflects the individual. In contrast, **structure** can also force **conformity** where individuals are made to fit into a given structure. This in turn gives rise to an inert, conformist culture.

In post-war Japan, in order to achieve high economic growth necessary for Japan to catch up with the rest of the world, an educational system devoted solely to enhancing the intellect developed. Such a policy, implemented through constant standardized testing, was thought to produce the types of people who would be able to move Japan quickly to new economic heights. While this was accomplished, the character and independence of individuals were suppressed and individuals were submerged into a society of **conformity**. The negative consequences of these educational policies have recently been playing out as the educational system as a whole has come under scrutiny.

The rise and fall of communism in the former Soviet Union also reflected the turn toward negative implications of **structure**. In order to provide a solution to the age-old problems of poverty and inequality, a national system to respect all individuals (or at least workers) was implemented. However, the **structure** ended up serving to suppress individuals and dissent to such an extent that the whole system fell apart from within.

The ability of humanity to bring about structures, whether educational or social, that, instead of suppressing individuals and forcing **conformity**, develop a sense of **pluralistic order** is something that remains an open question for the future.

Balance : Harmony or Stagnation

Balance in a positive sense involves everything being in their proper place providing a stable and balanced world, that is, in a word, **harmony**. But the **flow** and **circulation** of things stagnate, the **balance** in the world gets upset. This impulse is **stagnation**.

Recently in Japan, there has been a surprising increase in the number of late middle-age divorces of people who had been married for over 20 years. Often occurring after the husband's retirement, the couple who had, over those years, seemed to be in **balance**, in reality, never had a close relationship. In the absence of communication, they had maintained over a long period of time, a semblance of balance, but in fact their relationship had been cold and in **stagnation**. In fact, couples who argue among each other, while perhaps seeming not to be in **harmony**, may in fact be sharing their innermost feelings with each other. Indeed, such couples may at times have better relationships, where they argue out of respect for each other and communicate their feelings (**flow** and **circulation** of the self) with each other.

Eruption : Creation or Destruction

The force of **eruption** creates new things and events in the ever-evolving world, that is, **creation**. But the force of **eruption** can also devolve, when people go against the providence of nature, into **destruction**.

For example, humanity developed scientific technologies that allow the extraction of energies from natural resources such as oil, coal, or atoms. By doing so, humans have made possible a life style with a zone of comfort apart from the harsh aspects of nature. The **creation** of new medicines has also allowed humans to protect themselves from illness and to prolong life. The creative aspect of this vital force has also led to inventions such as communications networks which allow people to trade and communicate with each other.

But the force of **eruption** has also led to the invention of new weapons of mass **destruction** including nuclear weapons that can wipe out hundreds of thousands of people in an instant. The same technologies which were supposed to provide a better life style for us have also spun off destructive pollutants (including radioactive materials) that harm the environment. The force of **eruption** must thus be harnessed toward the **creation** of a more purified and improved world; otherwise, it will devolve into **destruction**.

The Six Forces Reflected in the Rise and Fall of Nations

The positive and negative aspects of the **six forces** can be seen in concrete examples such as the rise and fall of nation-states and civilizations. The Roman Empire might be a good example, especially in the **creation** of its arts and technology even as it fell from its height (**destruction**). Although it would be hard to pinpoint any single factor that accounts for its rise, one factor that gave it the force of **eruption** would be the social system in which those from a subordinate social rank could rise to positions of power. *The History of the Decline and Fall of the Roman Empire*, written by Edward Gibbon (1737-94), places the period of the five emperors as the height of the Roman Empire not only within Rome itself, but the nation-states under the rule of Rome. Throughout the empire, because of an **upward spiral** (the force of **circulation**) of prosperity, a comfortable level of living was established.

As with the saying, "All roads lead to Rome," the Romans were able to establish a network of highways that had Rome as its central "polis" or city. The **linkage** of roads led to **mutual interdependence**, while the force of this **structure** gave **order** to the Empire's stability and prosperity. However, its growth in this fashion meant **encroachment on others**. This negative impulse, while leading to a long period of stability, eventually led to **stagnation** of the empire because of the focus on **instant gratification** that became prevalent in a culture of **conformity**. All this sowed the seeds for the ultimate fall of the

Roman Empire at the hands of the Vandals after the fall of Carthage, which had previously been hard won for the Roman Empire by Scipio Africanus the Younger in the great siege of Carthage.

The Six Forces That Transform an Era 1 : The French Revolution
The **six forces** not only appear in the rise and fall of nations, but at times when nations and civilizations undergo a major transformation of their culture and society. Such transformations involve a radical shift in both values and social structure. A good example is the transformation of French society from an aristocratic one to a civil one in the eighteenth century.

In the period immediately preceding the French Revolution, power was held by the aristocrats who led extravagant lives and the clergy, which, in its special position in society, benefited inordinately. These two groups, while losing out in the increasingly capitalist society, held on to their status and power within the absolutist monarchy of French society. But this once-stable political culture entered **stagnation** because these groups in power simply dwelt in **conformity** and clung onto that system. Furthermore, the king's coffers were nearly depleted because of the annual payments to the privileged classes as well as to finance territorial wars. The depletion of funds coincided with the accumulation of great sums of debt which led the government to fall into a political **downward spiral**.

In contrast, those left out of the privileged classes were both the merchants (bourgeoise) who benefited from the new market-oriented culture and the peasants who toiled under increasingly unfavorable circumstances. The clash between the privileged and non-privileged groups became inevitable.

The individuals in the so-called Enlightenment movement were, in these conditions, able to highlight the need to correct the errors of the old feudal structure as well as the need to bring on a social revolution. The success of the American War of Independence also gave impetus to those who sought freedom from absolutist monarchies. The Declaration of the Rights of Man (to liberty, equality, and fraternity), which emerged during this time, envisioned a society of **harmony** and **mutual interdependence**. This new vision of society could not be contained within French borders and spread around the world as a **cre-**

ation of a new, more modern **order** of society.

This potential and hope of the French Revolution, however, was soon dashed. The insecure leaders of the Revolution **encroached on each other's** turf unable to trust anyone, sending people to their deaths at the guillotine. The positive light of the **six forces**, as can be clearly seen in this example, can be transformed into darkness.

The Six Forces That Transform an Era 2 : The Meiji Restoration

The positive and negative aspects of the **six forces** also appeared at an important turning point in Japanese history, the end of the so-called "closed nation" status in the late nineteenth century. The opening of Japan to a new era signaled the end of a 250-year-old feudal regime toppled by the leaders of several provinces in the periphery of western Japan. How did such a major transformation take place? The answer lies in the workings of the **six forces**.

All of the **six forces** were embedded in the conditions of the late nineteenth century, when the feudal regime, which had held power for so long, existed only in form and was rife with internal dissension. Those working for the regime were in a state of **stagnation**, while the new energies, that would impel the Meiji Restoration (1868), came from the provinces. Indeed, it is said that this major restructuring of the Japanese polity was directed by only 3,000 samurai from the provinces, which meant that the vast majority of samurai were mired in the old feudal structure, unable to recognize the momentous change that Japan was undergoing. Indeed, the rigidities of the feudal structure meant that the feudal government was also unable to respond rapidly to external pressures. The well-known Black Ships, led by the American Admiral Perry, turned out to be a catalyst to open Japan up to the rest of the world in terms of foreign relations and trade. Although the Japanese government knew of the coming of the Black Ships up to a year in advance, their rigidity meant that they were unable to prepare for their arrival. The end result was that Japan was forced to sign unfavorable trade and foreign relations treaties.

With foreign countries threatening from the outside and the provinces posing a threat from within, Japan in this period was at a turning point. Unless the government reacted appropriately and systematically, the whole structure would collapse under its own weight.

In this situation, the government was only able to respond on a hap-hazard basis (such as opening up a select number of ports upon demands from foreign powers), unable to do anything but seek **instant gratification** or temporary solutions. These half-hearted responses led to compromise after compromise both toward the provinces and to the foreign powers. This **downward spiral** eventually led to the collapse of the feudal regime. The old feudal system was governed by the **six negative conditions** which were overcome by the **six positive conditions** embodied in the new imperial government.

On the **upward spiral** were the rising energies of a new ideology that aimed to create a new **order**, to restore the emperor. A whole new polity, based on the forces of modernity, emerged when the new leadership acted jointly (**mutual interdependence**) to synergistically create a new Japan. A confluence of events and trends came together, including technological advances, new life styles, philosophies, and educational systems. Emerging in a new Western-style political framework, an **eruption** spread throughout the land. These energies that came together, forces that surpass any one individual, are just an instance of the workings of the cosmic **six forces**.

The Long Journey to Becoming a Supreme Bodhisattva

The Promise between the Human and the Universe

Although the **six forces** constitute the universe, the universe by itself cannot put them into action. In fact, the universe has assigned the human being to work with the forces of the universe. Humans are the only beings endowed by the universe with the ability and the responsibility to deal with both the positive and negative aspects of these **six forces**. The universe is thus not complete without humans, just as the human cannot exist without the universe. Originally, the universe made a promise to the human and vice versa that each would complete the other: the universe by providing the **six forces** and the human by putting them into action in the appropriate way.

The human and the universe thus exist as two distinct realms, but ultimately as one. However, during the 20th century, we humans have cut ourselves off from the universe, pretending as if we could exist without having to listen to the call of the universe. In the new millennium, the challenge we humans face is to make whole the two realms once again. If the 20th century was one of division created by human self-aggrandizement, the 21st century challenges us to listen to and resonate with the universe.

The Supreme Bodhisattva Responds to the Universe

To resonate to the call of the universe is to respond appropriately to the **six forces** that appear around us at all times. We must look at and listen deeply to the universe and ask ourselves what it is trying to convey to us. What is our purpose in life at this moment? How do we respond to our current situation? We must also ask these questions and use the **six forces** to positive ends by examining the relationship between our "self," our "world," and our "times" and deciding what is required of us.

In Buddhism, a being who is able to respond to the cries and calls of the universe is called a bodhisattva. Such a being, by correctly perceiving the situation and responding to it, is able to save all beings and enlighten the ignorance in the world, by combining both insight and a state of awakening. A supreme bodhisattva ties together the universe and us human beings.

In our present time, to respond to the challenge of the new millennium is akin to the ability of the supreme bodhisattva to naturally use the **six forces** to break down old barriers and find new solutions to current problems. The purpose of the **Grand Challenge** is for us to become supreme bodhisattvas of our time.

Records of the Grand Challenge

The Working of the Six Forces in Individual Situations

So far, we have discussed the workings of the **six forces** in the universe and in the broad scheme of human history, but the **six forces** are also at work on a more intimate, corporate or individual level such as at work, in the home, or within one's own heart. The task at hand is to understand the nature of the **six forces** as they work within our daily lives and to learn how to transform their energies into a positive direction and prevent their degeneration toward negativity.

Here we will take up the "records" or stories of the ways in which two individuals, both entrepreneurs, took up the Grand Challenge of working with the **six forces**. All the stories here use pseudonyms for the individuals.

A Record of an Individual's Grand Challenge I

The first individual is Mitsuko Kayama, age 64, who is the president of a trading company. Four years ago, when her husband passed away, it was beyond her wildest dreams that she would be a leader in the business world. Her husband had been an entrepreneur heading several businesses mainly in the fisheries industry. When the husband suddenly had a stroke and passed away, Ms. Kayama found herself at the helm of one of the businesses that her husband had managed.

Thrust into this role, her days were filled with seemingly unending problems as she had to deal with the numerous attempts by other members of the firm who were intent on taking over her former husband's position. Because of this, not only did the company's trading opportunities decrease with the loss of her able husband, but the morale within the company fell as the internal bickering continued. All of this was happening while the fisheries industry as a whole was undergoing a period of economic downturn, so her company was heading toward a certain bankruptcy. This situation forced Ms. Kayama to the brink, both financially as well as mentally.

Each day of the first year after she took over the company was like an emotional roller coaster. All the incidents that followed—the future of her company, its relationships with other companies, the morale of the employees—were an entanglement of light and darkness. Ms. Kayama's inner life was also a series of ups and downs with her daily life characterized by an utter inability to control her emotions.

It was very clear that the energies and forces that pushed her around every day were immense. Swayed by these forces, she was unable to grasp, let alone perceive what these energies were. And yet, "something" was palpably setting the course of her every thought and act. The "something" was none other than the **six forces** we have discussed thus far, which moved in positive directions at times, but certainly also acted to create negative consequences as well.

The force of **flow**, for instance, moved negatively in Ms. Kayama's company as everyone sought to take advantage of the situation of her

Darkness			Light	
The Law of Disintegration			**The Universal Principle of Integration**	
Isn't able to establish the firm's foundations at a critical point, which leads to bankruptcy.	Isn't able to go beyond each situation. Isn't able to deepen nor transmit insight.	**FLOW**	Not taken by traditional ways of doing things. Able to blaze a new approach and basis for challenging things.	Use critical junctures as opportunities to move toward a new and better direction.
Can't stop the negative cycle and the poor performance of the company.	Rules and methods that have been set are unconsciously followed.	**CIRCULATION**	Techniques and know-how based on deep insight take form.	Good cycles help propel other good business cycles.
Become influenced by the extreme ups and downs of one's surroundings.	Become dependent on or overbearing toward other companies.	**LINKAGE**	The company is able to resonate with other companies and mutually serve as good influences.	Able to create a company structure that is strong in both good and bad situations.
The individual is drowned within the organization, which becomes bland and lethargic.	A rigid hierarchical structure is created.	**STRUCTURE**	Everyone has a common mission and knows their role within it.	The company's potential is fully realized.
Challenges, blazing new paths, and spirit of service are all lost. Gradually the company disintegrates.	The attitude of "not rocking the boat" dominates and an extreme conservativism takes over.	**BALANCE**	An efficient and stable system is established.	A stable base is developed for further improvement.
Negative impacts are left to the world (environmental pollution, weapons, and negative ideologies).	Thinking only of short-term benefit, a long-range vision is lacking, leading to many problems.	**ERUPTION**	New technologies, methods, and products are created in relation to social needs.	Overcoming difficulties, fulfilling possibilities, and the development of society.

Chart 3 : The Working of the Six Forces in Individual Situations

husband's death. Seeking forms of **instant gratification**, the company began to degenerate toward bankruptcy, unable to develop good ideas. Thrust suddenly into such an anxiety-filled position, Ms. Kayama could only attempt short-term solutions herself. The negative force of **flow** led to the gradual disintegration of the whole structure of the company itself as the force of **circulation** also turned increasingly negative. The company fell into a **downward spiral** as old rules were only mechanically followed, while business went sour as trade deals fell through and employee morale fell to an all time low.

And because of the force of **linkage**, when the company declined in this fashion, relationships with other firms also soured. The weak internal situation led to overdependence on other companies as the other firms started to "encroach onto" Ms. Kayama's company. The link to others, moving negatively, meant that the power of the parent company (which was the largest stockholder in Ms. Kayama's company) grew increasingly larger and her firm increasingly weaker. Furthermore, since the fisheries industry as a whole was facing a financial crunch, that affected her company as well.

The negative turn of **flow, circulation, linkage** taken together moved the whole situation toward **destruction**. This destructive situation, which seemed to swallow up Ms. Kayama and her company, was the palpable energy that she experienced in the first year after she took over the company.

How to deal with this negative turn of events was the highest priority for Ms. Kayama at that time. Usually, when most of us are faced with a similar situation, the initial reaction might be to fret about it in such a manner that the fretting leads to total inaction. Or in contrast, we might get over-involved with the situation such that our zealous attempts to fix the situation actually lead to more problems. Unable to clearly perceive the actual situation (whether the external causes of the situation or problems with the internal reactions to it), we tend to be unable to act at all or fumble into the situation with a great deal of resolve, but without a clear course of action.

The turning point for Ms. Kayama was that she sensed that whatever the external situation might be, there was something within her own self that was connected to it and held the key to its resolution. This realization was crucial because whenever a major problem arises in our lives, the first step must be not to over-react to and get swallowed up in the particular situation.

For example, if person X has caused some problems in one's company, the usual thing to do is to blame him for the problems and see oneself as a victim of his actions. However, Ms. Kayama decided not to make this simplistic response of dividing problems into those who cause them and those who are victimized by them. Rather, she sought out answers to this situation and to this individual by looking within herself. She questioned why person X had come to act like this or whether there was something she could have done before X became this way. Interrogating herself in this fashion, she sought out the best approach to resolve the situation. Rather than being quick to find blame on the outside, she began an internal process of searching for answers.

She had confidence that if she found equanimity within herself so that she could find solutions from within, she could extend these solutions to the external problems. The confidence in this perspective that the central axis of action lies within removed her fear and gave her the courage and conviction to tackle each and every situation in which she found herself.

As she began this process, the negative dimensions of **flow**, **circulation**, and **linkage** began to slow down and the situation also started to show incremental signs of becoming positive. She tried to improve the overall atmosphere of the company, first by adopting a more flexible and open approach to each situation, which led to the force of **flow** turning positive. Taking **each moment as a precious moment**, she instilled a new company culture of seeing each situation as an opportunity to creatively think about new solutions. This openness gradually made for a much more positive setting for company business.

It was then that, like a miracle, help came from the outside for Ms. Kayama so that her company could operate more independently from the parent company. The force of **linkage** moved in a positive direction here in such a way that the company could stand in a healthy **mutual interdependence** with other firms and be flexible enough to build on good times, but also withstand bad times. All this led to an **upward spiral** (the positive force of **circulation**) in which as more positive building blocks were put in place, more positive things befell the company.

A Record of an Individual's Grand Challenge II

The next individual is Yoshio Takamatsu, age 50, who is the president of an electronic appliances manufacturer. Some years ago, his company was known to be hierarchically rigid and the employees never had any input into the management of the company. Furthermore, it seemed that every month there was someone who resigned their position in the company. Although he initially blamed "the outside" for this situation—whether it be the poor attitude of the employees or the lack of cooperation from the directors—he ultimately took it upon himself to look within himself for the causes of these problems.

One of these causes was his punctilious insistence on orderliness. For him, "problems" were a blight on his vision of an orderly company and so whenever any hint of a problem emerged, he ruthlessly pressured his employees to correct the situation. However, this led his employees to work in a state of fear and never be able to voice their own concerns and opinions about the direction the company was taking. His insistence on order meant that the force of **structure** moved negatively toward **conformity** and a lack of creativity within the company run from the top down. His vision of what gave **balance** to the company also meant that everyone exerted a great deal of effort to prevent "problems." However, what this led to was **stagnation** within the company and a complete lack of the pioneering spirit to challenge and render new services.

When Mr. Takamatsu realized that the problem with his company lay with him, he tried to change the company by changing himself. For starters, he tried to be more cheery. Although on a few occasions his face became contorted when he tried to force a smile, his enthusiasm and attempts to provide a more cheery atmosphere extended to his employees. His employees started to speak out at meetings and become more involving in giving shape to the company.

Mr. Takamatsu adopted the stance that when a problem occurred, it could be taken as an opportunity to try something new to further dialogue among the members of the firm. The negative movement of **structure** and **balance** was stopped, while the **flow** and **linkage** began activating. This combination led to the positive impulses of the **six**

forces, which led in turn each employee to take **each moment as a precious moment** and to be more flexible in their approach to every-day occurrences at the company. Everyone at the company started to share a common mission and concretely feel the positive energies of the **mutual interdependence** of all. Ultimately, what this led to was the almost complete lack of resignations from the company, which became a more efficient and stable firm.

In both Ms. Kayama and Mr. Takamatsu's cases, when they were drowned in the negativity of the **six forces**, they could not imagine the positive aspects at all. With all of us, as well, we must have the confidence that even in the darkest of situations, a positive, light-filled transformation is possible.

CHAPTER 2

A New Paradigm to Understand
the Inner and Outer Worlds

	Structure		Keywords
Chapter 1 The Path of Resonating with the Universe	The State of Enlightenment That Pervades All Things (The Underlying Theme)		Six Forces
Chapter 2 A New Paradigm to Understand the Inner and Outer Worlds	The State of Enlightenment (Ultimate Purpose)	The 21st Century The Other Side of the Faultline	Chaos Mind-and-Form Unit
Chapter 3 The Soul Compass	Causes of Suffering (Present Situation-Causes)	The 20th Century This Side of the Faultline	Four Blades
Chapter 4 The Inception of the Grand Challenge (To Look within Ourselves)	The Path (Method-Means)	From the 20th to the 21st Century (Transcending the Faultline)	To Look within Ourselves
Chapter 5 The Inception of the Grand Challenge (To Connect Our Inner Selves and the Outer World)			To Connect Our Inner Selves and the Outer World

Paradigm Shift

Tolstoy's Three Parables

In Chapter 1, we discussed the purposes of the **Grand Challenge** in terms of finding a way to positively resonate and respond to the **six forces** and to look deeply within for solutions to the problems we face. However, before we can concretely walk down this path, there is a fundamental obstacle—the way we perceive ourselves and our relationship to the world. In this chapter, we start with examining the fundamental premises of our relationship with the world and offer a new paradigm to understand the reality of this connection to the universe. We will use Leo Tolstoy's *Three Parables* as an entry point into exploring this new paradigm.

Parable 1 : The Story of the Farmer

Weeds had covered everyone's farmland. Though all the farmers helped each other cut the weeds, they always seemed to grow back right away. It was then that a good and wise lord told them that weeds needed to be taken out by their roots because simply cutting them, in fact, encouraged their growth. However, after some time, the lord's words were forgotten and people went back to simply cutting the weeds year after year.

However, after some time, there was someone who remembered part of the teaching about weeds and told everyone that they should stop cutting the weeds (forgetting the crucial part about taking out the roots). However, when the farmers stopped cutting the weeds, it was not surprising that weeds began to overrun the fields and made farming impossible. Thus the farmers came to look upon the person who gave the partial advice about not cutting the weeds as an evil person. They avoided him because they thought he was trying to take away their fields.

Parable 2 : The Story of the Merchant

There were a number of merchants who dealt in flour, butter, and milk. They all wanted to get rich quick and thus made up many different ways of making a larger profit, including mixing their products with cheaper ingredients which were not good for one's health. These products went from the wholesalers to retailers and from those retailers to others before finally ending up at the markets of the big cities. In the cities, however, since these doctored products were all that were available, however unsatisfied they might have been with the product, that was all they knew.

One day, a countrywoman who dealt with farm produce and always hand-prepared her meals went to the city. Immediately she picked up on the lack of quality in the farm produce in the city. When she started pointing this out to everyone, the merchants all accused her of telling people to abandon their produce, instead of focusing on the fact that what she was suggesting was a change to a better quality of produce. They started shouting to the crowds, "This woman is saying these things because she is poor and jealous. She is trying to get all of you to share her state of poverty and starvation. And indeed, if we stop selling these wares to you, you will all end up dying of starvation." The crowds, then, wildly condemned the woman.

Parable 3 : The Story of the Traveller

There were some travellers who came up upon some moorlands and thickets. They had to use their hands to get through the thicket undergrowth and thorn bushes to move forward. The travellers, at this point, divided up into two groups. One group claimed, "Our sense of direction is not wrong. As long as we continue going forward, we can get to our destination." The other group opined, "The direction we are going is wrong. We cannot continue here, but we need to spread out to find the right path." In other words, one group advocated going straight on and the other, spreading out in all directions.

But there was one traveller among them that said, "But surely we first need to stop to understand where we stand. We ought to use the sun and the stars as guides to our destination." However, people in the other groups had already made up their minds and were stubborn, so refused to listen to him, concluding that he was saying things like that because he was a coward and a derelict. As a result, neither of the two groups was able to reach their final destination and even today are wandering in the thick undergrowth and thickets.

The Three Ignorances : Ignorance of Causes, Truth, and Method
Each of the three parables above shows us something about the stupidity of human beings. The first story about the weeds teaches us about the "ignorance of causes" in which we cannot grasp the true cause or reason for a given situation. Instead of approaching the weed problem by looking beyond the soil surface to its roots, there is a tendency among humans to ignore what is not right in front of them. In the second story about the corrupt merchants, the parable compels us to think about the reality that we don't always know truth from falsehood. We humans have the tendency to think that what is presented to us as a given is the truth. In the story, the defective goods were tainted from the outset at the wholesale level, but after the goods were distributed down to the smallest retailer, it would have been hard to determine the true nature of the product. In such a way, the reality and the norms in which we live have been, to a certain extent, constructed by people from the past and we are sometimes unable to distinguish between reality and what has been constructed. And finally in the third story about the lost travellers, the lesson is surely about one of method. Even if the goal is clear, the path to that goal or the method to achieve the goal is sometimes unclear. People bring into their approaches all kinds of baggage which biases their perspectives. Unable to start from scratch, we humans often flounder in the process of finding the correct approach to a goal.

The three ignorances exemplified by the stories all point to the Buddhist analysis of problems:
1) Causes of Suffering (Present Situation-Causes)—Ignorance of the Causes of Suffering
2) Elimination of the Causes of Suffering (Enlightenment)—Ignorance of the Truth
3) The Path—Ignorance of the Method (to be free)

The "causes of suffering" describes the condition we are in (suffering) and analyzes its causes, while the "elimination of suffering" describes the condition we can potentially be in if we eliminate the causes of suffering (enlightenment). And "the path" prescribes the methods to fulfill the purpose of being free from suffering.

Thus in the first story, because people were unable to see the causes of the problems, they suffered. In the second story, being ignorant of the truth meant that they were unable to see the truth (be in a state of enlightenment). And in the third story, the floundering travellers represent the inability to lay out a path or method to reach the destined goal.

In order to rise to the **Grand Challenge** of the new millennium, we must become aware of these three limitations or ignorances (of causes, truth, and method). For if we are able to understand ourselves in this way, we will be able to build a bridge from the 20th to the 21st century, a movement from "suffering" to the "elimination of the causes of suffering," in other words, enlightenment, and "the path" to be taken for that end. This is the process which will be outlined in this book.

What Is Your View of the Inner and Outer Worlds?

The problems we face in every facet of our lives at this point in human history are not ones that can be solved piecemeal, but only in a wholistic and systematic manner. To attain the 21st-century goal of the "elimination of the causes of suffering," instead of focusing on particular problems, we must, first off, develop a critical way of thinking about all of our problems more broadly. To move in this direction requires not small steps, but a radical shift, a new paradigm for thinking about the relationship between the inner and outer worlds.

Until now, there have been those who absolutely denied a correlation between our inner thoughts, attitudes, and emotions with the outer, physical reality. To support this perspective on life, the gap between what we might inwardly desire and what actually faced us from the outside world would be highlighted. On the other hand, there have also been those who asserted an absolute unity between the inner and outer worlds wherein it was claimed the outer reality could be manipulated by the way we thought and felt. However, both these perspectives represent the old paradigm regarding the inner-outer relationship.

To Shift the Paradigm

Imagine if you will that you are in a large, pitch-dark room where you have dropped a key. You get on your hands and knees to try to find this small object on the floor, but the space you need to cover is quite spacious. As can be imagined, this would be quite a cumbersome task and you might think of more efficient methods to help find the key such as going through the room more quickly or inviting a number of people to assist in the search.

However, an approach that actually goes to the source of the problem—the lack of illumination—would be a shift in the problem-solving paradigm. Instead of focusing on the lost key, one ought to search for a way to illuminate the room, either by turning a light switch on or by some other means, for that is the real cause of why the key could not be located. To shift one's paradigm, then, means to think about problems in a radically new way. More broadly speaking, for us to face up to the problems of the world today, we must also start thinking about them in a fresh manner. Here, I will take up two new paradigm shifts: 1) learning to see how **chaos can be divided into light and darkness** and 2) **the reality created by our mind-and-form unit**.

The Human Who Can Divide Chaos into Light and Darkness

Inside the Repetition of Things
Every day we are faced with numerous daily happenings. Whether it be incidents in the family—involving spouses, mothers- and daughters-in-law, or the children—we all have events happen where we lose confidence in what we are meant to do. For entrepreneurs, it could be company meetings or new business proposals that call on them to respond appropriately. In any arena, our lives are a constant barrage of happenings which demand our full attention and appropriate response. Depending on our way of dealing with these events, the course of things changes dramatically.

What Is Chaos?
The term **chaos** is used here not to refer to the antithesis of "order," but rather to mean the ambiguous and unfixed reality of the world before human beings attempt to order it. Although humans construct realities like up and down or good and bad, Buddhists have long pointed to a reality that exists prior to such human ordering. **Chaos**, therefore, is the reality before human intervention which appears before us moment by moment. We humans thus react to this **chaos** by trying to construct and give shape to this unformed reality.

A block of wood, for example, is "chaotic" in the sense that before human intervention, it exists as itself, full of potential to take any number of shapes. A wood carver might shape a Buddhist statue out of it or something completely secular. The block of wood can also be combined with fire or water to create something completely different. This limitless potential of original reality (**chaos**) means that **chaos** simultaneously exists as such and in potential to become something else.

An Ability Given to Humans : To Divide Chaos into Light and Darkness

A characteristic of the human, as opposed to other species, is that when faced with this "chaotic" reality, we have the ability to draw out of it both light and darkness. This is because **chaos** has embedded within itself the potential for both positive and negative consequences.

For example, human beings have been skilled in the past centuries in drawing out, from the natural world, "energies" that have served our interests. We have been able to make the dark night light in our rooms with electricity or make those same rooms comfortable temperature-wise whether in winter or summer. Convenient applications such as televisions or vehicles such as cars or airplanes have also been born from the human ability to draw out positive functions from the mater-ial world. However, this same ability has also drawn out negative con-sequences such as the atomic bomb, which even with its use just twice in World War II, has resulted in prolonged anguish for many victims.

The original reality of **chaos**, for example the piece of wood, would have remained just as it was, were it not for human intervention with this reality. The consequence of this interaction, however, was the pro-duction of both positive and negative results for both humans and the world at large.

We Can No Longer Return to Chaos

One fundamental principle in the universe is that once the formless, chaotic reality is shaped by humans, it can never return to its original state. For example, if we take the case of the atomic bomb, even if we wanted to return to an era "before the bomb," once invented, we can-not un-invent it. However much we might regret having brought a

Figure 1 : The Human Who Can Divide Chaos into Light and Darkness

new phenomenon into the world, we cannot erase it to go back to a prior time.

Especially in the 20th century, the ability of human beings to create and form new scientific advances (both positive and negative) out of the formless **chaos** has speeded up to such an extent that these new creations have much greater and more complex impact than any other time in human history. Given that humans are the only species to have this power to choose between light and darkness, we must become more self-aware of our responsibility to use this power properly as well as discern the threats that we can put upon ourselves and the world with this ability.

This discussion of **chaos** is not something that is abstract and removed from our daily lives. Indeed, our everyday existence is suffused with the constant bombardment of this chaotic reality to which we each try to give order and meaning, both consciously and unconsciously. Although we might regret some of the ways in which we reacted and gave form to the limitless potential of **chaos**, it is only with the privilege of hindsight that we are able to say this. If only we could have foresight into the nature of all the events and happenings that we would face, might we be better able to respond to it. The study of the nature of **chaos**, thus, serves us well as we reflect on how we ought to best respond to it.

How to Shape Chaos Positively

The 21st century exists for us today only as a future potential. However, whether we like it or not, this formless reality (**chaos**) will shift from the future to the present in a very short period of time. How we respond to this potential reality will shape the course of the future, whether positively or negatively. We must practice a path, an inner discipline, to be able to resist the negative dimensions of **chaos** and draw out the positive dimensions.

If you imagine a white plate with an equal amount of black and yellow paint and mix them together, you would end up with a chaotic assemblage of color (Figure 2). Trying to resist the negative aspects of **chaos** and draw forward the positive aspects is akin to trying to separate out the black and yellow paint once they have been mixed together. We humans have not sufficiently developed our insight and state of

Figure 2 : The Image of Chaos

awakening to perform such a task. However, there is hope. The **Grand Challenge** is precisely a challenge to ourselves to endeavor to creatively come up with a radically new paradigm to solve problems of a much greater magnitude that the entire world faces.

The Mind-and-Form Unit : A New Awareness of the Inner and Outer Worlds

Nihilism and Egoism

So far we have discussed the idea of the human choosing the darkness or the light of **chaos**. But another paradigm for the new millennium is the idea that reality is created from an interaction between the inner and outer worlds. Before we discuss our new vision of this relationship, we ought to review the older paradigms. There have been two perspectives which have dominated our understanding of the relationship between the inner and outer worlds.

The first is a view of the world in which there is a sense that no matter what one does, the world is so fraught with problems, that one is unable to do anything about it at all. This is a form of **nihilism**. People who subscribe to this point of view might think that those who believe that the mind or inner world can affect the course of the phenomenal world are simply idealist dreamers. In other words, from the nihilistic perspective, the phenomenal, outer world is the only real thing while our inner worlds are basically void of reality. The opposite perspective is one in which the human being is thought to be able to shape and form the world at will. This is a form of **egoism**. Although these two perspectives seem to be in direct opposition to each other, in fact they share common assumptions about the relationship between the inner and outer worlds that are mistaken.

The Mind-and-Form Unit

They are mistaken because the inner and outer worlds are related to each other, but not in a simplistic way. Here, we will take up the true nature of the relationship between the inner and outer worlds by focusing on the teaching of **mind-and-form unit**.

The word **form** is taken from Buddhism, which teaches that the world is constructed by both material or phenomenal "forms" and the

Figure 3* : Faces or a Goblet?

*Rubin's goblet-profile figure

underlying "emptiness" which characterizes all formless things such as the human mind or spirit. The word **mind** is the equivalent of the Buddhist "emptiness," that is to say, our inner world. In other words, the **mind-and-form unit** implies the inseparability of our outer (form) and inner (mind) worlds, which are bundled together as a set. They are so closely interconnected that, in fact, **mind** and **form** are actually one thing.

We might even say, "In the beginning was the **mind-and-form unit**." The interdependence of mind and form is illustrated in Figure 3 where some people might see a white goblet, while others might see two black silhouettes facing each other. For those who see the faces, the white goblet serves as a backdrop, while for those who see the goblet, the black regions fade away as background. But in reality, one needs to be there for the other to exist. The goblet allows the faces to appear, while the faces give definition to the goblet. In this way, the relationship between mind and form can never be separated. They need to be thought of as a unitary set, mutually interdependent on each other.

If we imagine **mind** and **form** as two rope strands (as pictured in Figure 4), they are wrapped over and around each other so that they are tightly entangled. **Mind** and **form** are not two.

An Experiment Regarding the Mind-and-Form Unit

To understand the concept of the mind-and-form unit, let us conduct a brief experiment. What do you see in Figure 5? In fact, this illustration contains two figures. On the one hand, it is possible to see an old haggard woman, but on the other a young, aristocratic-looking woman. In the course of my lectures on the **mind-and-form unit**, where I have used this illustration, the audience seems to be equally divided regarding which figure strikes them (see Figure 6 for a closer look at the two possible images).

What is interesting was that almost no one simultaneously saw both the old and young women. For those to whom an old woman appeared, it was very hard to see the young figure, and vice versa. When this experiment was conducted at an American university, the discussions that followed between the two groups that saw different images proved fascinating. Each group tried to convince the other of

Figure 4 : The Author Demonstrating the Entanglement of Mind and Form

what the correct image was. And only over time, were people convinced of the existence of other image in the illustration and perceived it. What this simple experiment suggests is that the biases that we hold within (mind) help to shape how we perceive the world (form) to be.

Immediate Feeling, Perception, Thoughts, and Action

How then does our mind work? There are basically four steps to our thought process: **immediate feeling, perception, thoughts, and action** (see Figure 7). Our mind takes in the phenomenal world (forms) through these four steps and conversely acts upon the world. The cycle of the world acting on our mind and our mind acting on the world has been repeated thousands, no, millions of times. This cyclical process of reality-formation demonstrates the inseparability of mind and form.

To explain this process more concretely, let us look at Figure 8, which depicts a woman standing at the edge of a cliff. Different people might have different thought processes on seeing this picture. One person might think that the woman is contemplating suicide and take the action to call the police for help. Another person might think that with the grand view of nature in the backdrop, it would make for a nice picture, and act to take a photograph. Or another reaction might be to fleetingly take notice of the person and not act in any particular way. In other words, faced with the same situation, depending on the state of our individual "minds," the way we react to "forms" from the world is completely different. The cycle of **immediate feeling, perception, thoughts, and action** that informs our thought processes acts on the world of forms in such a way that each of us develops different types of **mind-and-form units**.

Let us try another experiment. Figure 9 was an illustration handed out at one of our seminars. The instructions for this experiment were to team up into groups of three with the idea that the first person (the group leader) would be shown the original illustration and would then have to draw it as closely as possible for the second person who had not seen the picture. Finally, the second person would draw it as closely as possible for the final participant in the group to draw. The resulting picture was then matched with the original to see how closely they resembled each other. The only twist was that some groups were told

Figure 5* : The Mind-and-Form Unit—Experiment 1

*"My Wife and My Mother-in-Law" by W. E. Hill

Figure 6 : Experiment 1 Results

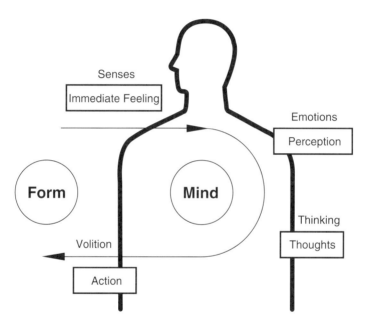

Figure 7 : Immediate Feeling, Perception, Thoughts, and Action

Figure 8 : A Woman Standing at the Edge of a Cliff

Figure 9 : The Mind-and-Form Unit—Experiment 2

Duck Figure   **Rabbit Figure**

Figure 10 : Experiment 2 Results –Rabbit Figure and Duck Figure

that Figure 9 was supposed to be a picture of a rabbit and others that it was a picture of a duck.

As can be seen in Figure 10, groups who were told it was a rabbit started to draw their pictures to resemble a rabbit, while those who were told it was supposed to be a duck, drew duck-like figures as the illustration got further away from the original. In other words, people who were told it was a rabbit or conversely a duck, sensed and acknowledged immediately that the picture shown to them by the group member preceding them was what they were told. They then thought about it before taking the action to reduplicate the image they held in their minds.

The Chemical Reaction of the Inner and Outer Worlds

The way in which the inner and outer worlds interact is very similar to a chemical reaction. For example, when hydrogen (H) reacts with oxygen (O), the compound H_2O or water can be created. However, the same hydrogen atom, when combined with chlorine (Cl), produces a very different substance, hydrochloric acid (HCl). In a similar fashion, the way in which we react to the world produces many different experiences.

Therefore the ways in which we have fashioned a reality for ourselves (our **mind-and-form unit**) have been based on countless such reactions involving the four steps of the thought process. This thought process, built up over a long time (which means that it is not easily changed), is something that we must come to understand about ourselves if we are to properly grasp the nature of both our inner and outer worlds.

To Reunite the Inner and Outer Worlds

Let's return to the question from which we started this chapter, that is, how we should understand the relationship between the inner and outer worlds. We have noted that although the old paradigms of nihilism and egoism seem fundamentally at odds, in fact, they share the common premise that the "inner" (mind) and "outer" (the world of forms) worlds are distinct and separable. However, we have shown here that the inner and outer worlds are inseparably interconnected through the **mind-and-form unit** which involves a process of reunit-

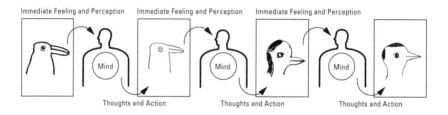

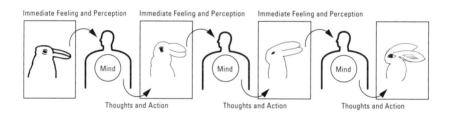

Figure 11: The Reality Created by the Mind-and-Form Unit and "Immediate Feeling, Perception, Thoughts, and Action"

Figure 12 : A Scene from a Lecture on the Mind-and-Form Unit

ing the mind and the world. The premise of our **Grand Challenge** is to understand a new two-fold paradigm: first, **the human being who separates chaos into light and darkness**, and second, **the reality formed by the mind-and-form unit**.

Records of the Grand Challenge

A Record of an Individual's Grand Challenge III

Now, let us take up the story of a medical doctor who managed to incorporate the teachings of the two new paradigms in his life. Naoyuki Yamauchi, age 43, is the head of the pediatrics ward of a general hospital. Taking care of children on a daily basis, he had earned the respect of colleagues and patients alike because of his care and professionalism.

When Dr. Yamauchi was in his middle and high school years and trying to decide his future, Japan was in the midst of its highest growth period. However, with that growth, came problems such as the explosion in the cases of thalidomide babies and outbreaks of the Minamata disease, caused by environmental pollutants from Japan's leading industries. Dr. Yamauchi could not but wonder what was to be done about these emerging problems.

Although he was not inclined toward the hard sciences, but rather as an avid reader thought he might find work in the arts and humanities, he was inspired by the acceptance of the Nobel prize in physics by Shinichiro Tomonaga. In this new age of scientific progress, he began to wonder if the old adage "The pen is mightier than the sword" was simply a piece of fanciful fiction that no longer could serve the current era. Instead, with the phrase "Possess nuclear weapons to deter nuclear weapons" becoming ever more popular, he thought to enter the hard sciences as he thought this new trend would be the best way to address social and environmental injustices such as the diseases mentioned above.

What could be a more suitable occupation than a doctor to most directly touch the lives of those who had undergone such injustices, thought Dr. Yamauchi. Angering his high school advisor by changing his major so close to university entrance exams, he stubbornly sought out his life's vision by studying to become a doctor.

Although he entered the medical profession with high ideals and hopes of solving environmental and other socially-caused diseases, he was soon faced with a depressing and hard real life of a doctor. He had to meet patients with chronic heart conditions one day only to find them dead the next. Last-stage cancer patients and those afflicted with mental illness were realities that he had not imagined. Indeed, all he could think of was the meaning of life itself as he saw that life was followed by certain death and he wondered what followed that death. This introspective side of Dr. Yamauchi caused him endless sleepless nights and drained his psyche of all its youthful vitality.

This was when he found that he could not deal with any of the specialty wards with the exception of the children's pediatrics ward. Although he had not particularly chosen to enter that department, he found that it was the most bearable of the specializations he could have chosen because most of the children were not quite as ill as adults in other wards and they seemed more cheerful. However, even here, a cold reality hit Dr. Yamauchi. As time went on, he had to be witness to these children dying from leukemia, cancer, and other life-threatening diseases that the children were born with. Their deaths seemed even harder because they were children and because of all the sadness that went along with death at such a young age, not only for the child but for the families involved.

This reality of pain and suffering in the hospital setting thus did not disappear just because he moved to the pediatrics ward. Faced with such suffering, he felt overwhelmed and each day he lost confidence and vitality. The certainty of death, no matter how hard he tried, left Dr. Yamauchi not only with a lack of confidence or trust in himself, but a lack of trust in the world which imposed such a reality. In concrete terms, he started to mistrust his own instincts as well as other people.

Not trusting others instilled in him a feel of always falling victim to others. Seeing the world and others as unfair, this feeling of victimization left him upset with everyone at the hospital. Thus his ability to relate to others seemed to be on the constant decline.

These feelings all came to a head in one incident when a four-year-old girl that he had attempted his best at treating, nevertheless, passed away from acute brain disease resulting from influenza. This little girl had come to the hospital with a slight fever and symptoms of a common cold. Dr. Yamauchi treated her for these symptoms and she was able to return home that day. However, that very evening she had an attack of convulsions and was immediately brought back to the hospital. By morning, the girl was unable to breathe on her own and several days later, she passed away after all treatments failed.

The girl's mother, in particular, was devastated by this turn of events and held very strong feelings of antipathy toward Dr. Yamauchi. These strong feelings finally ended up with the girl's family taking Dr. Yamauchi to court. Especially because the mother had previously always insisted that he was the one that was best qualified to look after their daughter and always insisted on his availability, being sued was an earth-shattering development for him. This was truly like **chaos** swirling all around him. How he would face this situation—what kind of **mind-and-form unit** he would adopt—could change the entire course of events.

As the trial date approached, all Dr. Yamauchi could think of was how unfair this whole situation was despite his best efforts at treating the girl. His anger at the unfairness of the trial even prompted him to consider a counter-suit to defend his name. He tried to give shape to the **chaos** around him by adopting a **mind-and-form unit** which could be called a **Resentful Victim**'s mentality.

The victim mentality tends to look for unfairness when there is none, turn perfectly innocent things into oppressive things, or otherwise tend toward taking a negative view of any and all events. Dr. Yamauchi, the girl's parents, and the hospital all seemed to be wrapped up in this victim mentality. It was in this context that I met Dr. Yamauchi and encouraged him to understand how this victim mentality worked and to reflect on his original intentions when he decided to become a doctor. After a lengthy process of discussions with him, we managed to clear up what needed to be given absolute priority and what could be discarded. As matters began to be clarified, he was able to approach this whole situation with a new mentality altogether.

His new attitude began with accepting the situation as it was. Including the withdrawal of the counter-suit, he decided upon a course of action that would not involve criticizing the opposing party. Although his lawyer wanted him to take a firm and critical stance

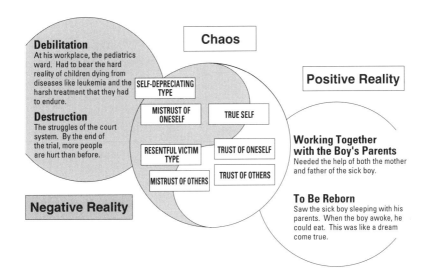

Chaos

Debilitation
At his workplace, the pediatrics ward. Had to bear the hard reality of children dying from diseases like leukemia and the harsh treatment that they had to endure.

SELF-DEPRECIATING TYPE

MISTRUST OF ONESELF

TRUE SELF

Destruction
The struggles of the court system. By the end of the trial, more people are hurt than before.

RESENTFUL VICTIM TYPE

TRUST OF ONESELF

MISTRUST OF OTHERS

TRUST OF OTHERS

Negative Reality

Positive Reality

Working Together with the Boy's Parents
Needed the help of both the mother and father of the sick boy.

To Be Reborn
Saw the sick boy sleeping with his parents. When the boy awoke, he could eat. This was like a dream come true.

Chart 4 : Dr. Yamauchi's Two Mind-and-Form Units

against the girl's family, at trial, all he said was, "Although we were unable to save her, we tried our very best." He saw the force of **destruction** in having a victim mentality as he recognized that court trials, by nature, tend to produce more victims by the end of the trial than at its beginning. He vowed to stop this cycle of victimization. In the end, the trial, which brought the truth to light, demonstrated that Dr. Yamauchi and the entire hospital staff had not only done anything wrong, but did their very best in attending to this particular patient.

At the conclusion to this entire incident, Dr. Yamauchi was able to reflect on the tremendously destructive power of **chaos** (in the form of a victim mentality) as he saw how much a counter-suit would have hurt the parents who had already gone through enough pain with the loss of their daughter.

But six years later, an astonishingly similar incident came upon Dr. Yamauchi. With an eerie sense of premonition, a young boy who had come in with cold symptoms had developed a life-threatening condition by nightfall after he had been sent home. Dr. Yamauchi had flashbacks to the incident with the girl. Although he had momentary doubts about if and how to explain the boy's condition to his parents, he knew that he needed their help and cooperation if they were going to overcome this illness. He explained to them that, in his experience, this condition would improve given time. While it was true that he did think so medically, he also needed to tell himself this psychologically to urge himself on to find a proper course of treatment.

Though in the earlier case with the girl, he had told the parents about the possible side effects of the treatment as a form of "informed consent," this time he also told the boy's parents that he would be fine. Although he had taken a different course of action the last time—to protect himself from later accusations of incompetence—on this occasion, he put himself on the line. He became willing to accept full responsibility for patients under his care. He knew that this was the right thing to do as long as he tried his very best and left the rest up to God.

He trusted that the parents would be understanding if he conveyed to them his sincere efforts. But what this trust was really about was his regaining a trust in himself and thereby being able to trust others as well. Six years ago, Dr. Yamauchi had a radically different attitude toward life, that of a lack of trust in both the self and others. What a difference six years made.

This positive approach made all the difference as he and the parents worked hard together to care for the child over a period of three days. It was like a dream when on the fourth day, Dr. Yamauchi saw the parents and the child fast sleep, after which the boy was able to eat normally. When the mother of the boy told him after the whole ordeal was over that she hadn't worried because she trusted him, it hit Dr. Yamauchi just how much things had changed over the course of the six years. By developing a new attitude, a new **mind-and-form unit**, he was able to experience such a radical transformation in the course of events.

Dr. Yamauchi's original intention in becoming a medical doctor was to develop the force and skills necessary to make a difference in a world of injustice. During the course of the six years, he was able to acquire such a force, a force for living wholeheartedly, that changed the course of events.

Although he had gone into science with the notion that it represented the "sword" (brute strength) or a force greater than the "pen" (the arts), he ultimately attained a force beyond both. This ultimate force is the human ability, as Dr. Yamauchi's **Grand Challenge** record illustrates for us, to face chaotic reality head on and shift its negative orientations toward the positive.

CHAPTER 3

The Soul Compass

	Structure		Keywords
Chapter 1 The Path of Resonating with the Universe	The State of Enlightenment That Pervades All Things (The Underlying Theme)		Six Forces
Chapter 2 A New Paradigm to Understand the Inner and Outer Worlds	The State of Enlightenment (Ultimate Purpose)	The 21st Century The Other Side of the Faultline	Chaos Mind-and-Form Unit
Chapter 3 The Soul Compass	Causes of Suffering (Present Situation-Causes)	The 20th Century This Side of the Faultline	Four Blades
Chapter 4 The Inception of the Grand Challenge (To Look within Ourselves)	The Path (Method-Means)	From the 20th to the 21st Century (Transcending the Faultline)	To Look within Ourselves
Chapter 5 The Inception of the Grand Challenge (To Connect Our Inner Selves and the Outer World)			To Connect Our Inner Selves and the Outer World

To Follow the Universal Principle of Integration

In the Midst of the Complexity of the Inner and Outer Worlds
In the previous chapter, we outlined two new paradigms that will help guide us in the new millennium: the human task of **turning chaos toward the positive** and the notion that **reality is constructed by our mind-and-form unit**. This process also involves two aspects. The first is to heighten our ability **to look within ourselves**, that is, to gain the wisdom to distinguish between the light and darkness within our inner selves, and the second is to develop a keen sense of how **to connect our inner selves and the outer world**, in other words, to understand our individual **mind-and-form units**.

But to actually look within ourselves is not as easily done as said. Most of us have not been taught how to look within ourselves and we can only understand our "mind" in an abstract or fuzzy way. Though we might understand what it means **to look within ourselves** on an abstract level, it is hard to concretely say what such a practice really involves. Our inner worlds are complex and unfathomable for most of us. Even as we try to look introspectively, we keep on coming up against new and unexpected things. It is as if we are exploring a dark forest in pitch darkness or trying to sail a small raft in the raging seas.

Conversely, our outer realities are equally complex. Things don't stay still for even a moment as we try to grasp the nature of our outer world. Thus, the different, but equally complex nature of both our inner and outer worlds provides us with a challenge as we try to come to terms with them. Indeed, the path of the **Grand Challenge** is to examine the intersection of these two worlds, our **mind-and-form units**.

What the Captains Ought to Have Done
There were four ship captains heading for a long sea voyage. Though they all set out for the same destination, none of them actually arrived. The first captain gave up on the journey when he saw the ill-prepared state of the ship and the uncooperative crew. Not expecting the rough waves, he gave up soon after the journey began. The second captain was a much more forceful man, ordering the ship to turn right when he felt like going right and turning left, when he felt like that. In the

end, the captain and his crew arrived, but at a completely different location. The third captain was a carefree fellow, who let the ship be guided naturally. Letting the winds carry them to whatever destination, his ship ultimately wandered aimlessly without ever reaching the goal. Finally, the fourth captain was an impatient man who cursed at the heavy winds during squalls and cursed at the lack of winds when the seas were calm. His temper got the best of him and his ship when they tried a dangerous maneuver and were shipwrecked.

Each captain took a course of action that matched their personalities and that they thought was the best approach. But ultimately, none of them were able to reach the final destination. What, then, were the captains to have done? What would you have done if you were the captain? When embarking on a long sea voyage, each captain should be aware that there is a prescribed route that they ought to take to ensure arrival. Although it is invisible, since there is terrestrial magnetism, each captain ought to have used a compass that could have guided them toward the goal.

This route or path to get to the goal is constantly being conveyed to us. What we need in our own journey is an accurate compass that will get us to the destination. Rather than be guided by what we know or presume, the compass should be our guide.

The Universal Principle of Integration

Our lives are like the vast oceans faced by the captains. Ahead of us will certainly be obstacles and rough waves that will complicate our journey. But do we also receive a magnetic pull for our lives?

Indeed, in our lives we are constantly being taught and redirected by events that tell us, "Be still, don't go there," "Now is the time to act" and so on. Within ourselves, we have the power and ability to listen to and heed these voices. Just as terrestrial magnetism works anywhere in the world, the world conveys directions to us at all times and places through what I call the **universal principle of integration** (the divine force).

The world calls out for integration, that is to make things whole or realize harmony, whether we recognize it or not. In the same way that terrestrial magnetism existed as an intangible force undetectable until humans invented the compass, the **universal principle of integration** exists and has always existed, but we have not had the proper **soul compass** to understand it until now. When we use this **soul compass,** we can finally arrive at the destination that life beckons to us. As we **look within ourselves** and **connect our inner selves and the outer world**, thus forming our authentic **mind-and-form units**, the **soul compass** constantly provides us with directions on how to accomplish this.

The Wisdom of the Soul Compass I : The Power to Look within Ourselves

The True Self and the False Self

The first and basic insight of the **soul compass** is to give us an orientation to the complex morass that is within our minds. It provides us with the power **to look within ourselves**. How is our inner world structured? A fundamental organization of our "self," that we must recognize, is the difference between the true self and the false self.

The **true self** lies at the heart of our inner world. This "soul" of our lives is the light which contains both love and insight, a place where the **universal principle of integration** can be responded to. Since this is our **true self**, this self needs to be recognized and liberated in order to be able to connect our selves with the world and truly resonate with the **six forces** that make up the world.

Unfortunately, if we grow up without recognizing and liberating this self, as most of us do, this **true self** develops a thick veil around it, not permitting its inner light to shine through. The veil is what can be called the **false self**, which, as will be explained in more detail below, is made up of four different types: **Over-Confident**, **Resentful Victim**, **Self-Depreciating**, and **Self-Satisfied**. These **four personality types** or orientations develop as we grow up unconscious of the true self. They exert a strong influence on how we see ourselves, but are based on basic delusions about the nature of the self and of the world. These **four personality types**, in contrast to the light-filled reality of our souls, represent the dark, negative energies that shift the chaotic reality toward negative ends.

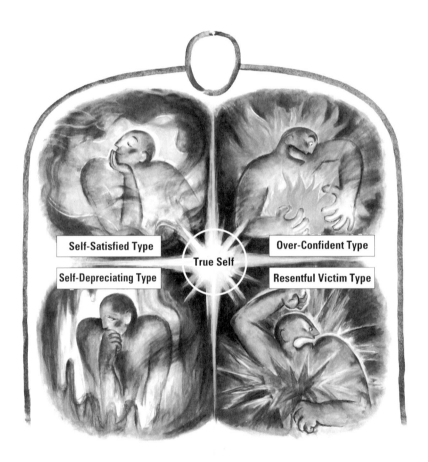

Figure 13 : The True Self and the Four Personality Types of the False Self

The Four Personalities of the False Self

To understand how these **four personality types** (see Figure 13) function more concretely, let us use a scenario in which different people with the different personality types are named to lead a project within a company. With the **Over-Confident** type, a person might view such a scenario as a great opportunity to move up in the company and demonstrate his abilities. Such a personality has an inflated sense of self-worth and is brimming with confidence, even though nobody else shares such an evaluation. With the **Resentful Victim** type, even when given such a chance, he is constantly worried about being a victim of good fortune. Always anxious and unable to trust others, his reaction might be to constantly be suspicious about other people's intentions and inclined to hurt others before they can hurt him.

In the case of the **Self-Depreciating** type, the immediate reaction would be to think that he is unworthy of such an opportunity and that other people would probably not trust him in such a leadership role. Thinking that others are probably making fun of him behind his back, he would regret ever taking on such a challenge and would try to find ways to run away from the chance. Finally, in the case of **Self-Satisfied** type, to have received this opportunity would in itself be seen as an accomplishment. Hoping to maintain his newfound position by getting along with everyone on his project team, he is satisfied with any existing reality. In contrast to the **Over-Confident** type who would see such an opportunity as simply a stepping stone to further achievements in the future, the **Self-Satisfied** type is satisfied with any and all situations. As can be seen with this simple scenario, these **four personality types** have rather different ways of accepting and responding to the world, which clearly lead to their creating different sets of realities.

Two Axes That Tint the Inner World

These **four personality types** in the inner world do not appear haphazardly, but rather, symbolize our inner darkness. Furthermore, two axes divide the four personalities into distinct types. These two axes are 1) the **Pleasure-Pain Axis** and 2) the **Recklessness-Lethargy Axis** (see Chart 5).

Pleasure and pain can generally be thought of as being determined by external factors. However, the same set of external factors might

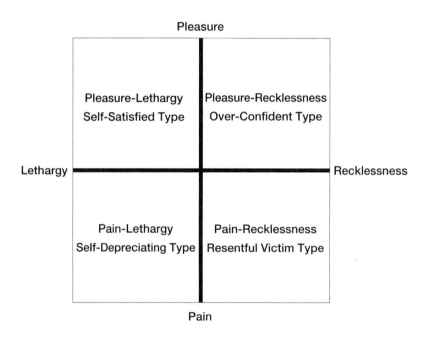

Chart 5 : The Two Axes and Four Personalities

receive completely different reactions from different people. On the one hand are people who are high on the **Pleasure Axis**, who would take whatever external factors in a positive and optimistic way and always see the greener side of the pasture. On the other, there are people high on the **Pain Axis**, who would react to the same factors pessimistically and always see the negative side of things. In other words, whether we have a personality type high or low on the **Pleasure-Pain Axis** determines how we will take things.

The **Recklessness-Lethargy Axis** refers to the internal factors that propel one to react to things with energy (**Recklessness**) or a lack of energy (**Lethargy**). In other words, those with a strong orientation toward **Recklessness** will react to events in the world powerfully and with an almost excessive energy. On the other hand, those tending toward **Lethargy** react passively or weakly toward the world, lethargically retreating into their own shell.

Though many people have the preconception that human ignorance erupts in violence or other forms of energy generated from the dark side of the human, such energies can also take more passive forms such as apathy or conformity. Thus, whether the energy is reckless or lethargic, we can understand the negative orientations of the human by looking at the various ways in which such energies are manifested (compare for instance, the right and left side of the diagram in Chart 5).

Thus with the **four personality types** and the different ways they manifest themselves along the two axes described above, we can map out a more precise typology of the human, namely: **Pleasure-Recklessness (Over-Confident Type)**; **Pleasure-Lethargy (Self-Satisfied Type)**; **Pain-Recklessness (Resentful Victim Type)**; and **Pain-Lethargy (Self-Depreciating Type)**.

The Universality of the Four Types

Throughout human history, our inner world has been described in many different ways. For example, in Buddhism, the keyword of inner darkness or unhealthy desires has been used as the generic framework for very detailed analyses of the human mind. I am also interested in the complex nature of the human mind and have developed the **four personality types** of the **false self** noted above to describe it. Here, let us examine more closely the various ways in which the four types interact.

In traditional Japanese culture, human emotions were divided into four types as well: joy, anger, sadness, and comfort (see Chart 6). Joy can be correlated with **Pleasure-Recklessness**. Although there is a type of joy that comes from the **true self**, the joy mentioned here is twisted into a self-centered joy based on winning something or from self-aggrandizement in an **Over-Confident** personality type.

Anger is an emotion closely associated with **Pain-Recklessness**. Those with a **Resentful Victim** personality type are often full of anger and resentment about the unfairness of the world. This anger is frequently vented against others and is prone toward destruction. In a similar way, sadness is associated with **Pain-Lethargy** while comfort is linked to **Pleasure-Lethargy**.

However, emotions like joy, anger, sadness, and comfort are important human feelings which ought not to be ignored. Indeed, they all have their gradations and subtypes. For example, there can be the type of anger one feels after having been hurt that is an outburst of rage that aims for revenge, or, a slow smoldering, even sad, type of anger that is hard to put into words. Furthermore, any of these emotions can be of a higher and true quality when they come from the **true self** or soul. Thus, these emotions, such as anger born of love, have a wide range of quality and meaning, and thus must be differentiated, though in Chart 6 they ought to be associated with the lower-level emotions of our **false self**.

There is another correlation that we can make between the **four personality types** and traditional classifications of human emotions. In traditional Buddhism, for example, it is said that when Shakyamuni Buddha sat under the bodhi tree to achieve enlightenment, the evil deity Mara, afraid of seeing the Buddha attain awakening, sent eight "armies" of emotions as weapons to veer the Buddha away from the path. They include: 1) the feeling of limitless craving (Greed), 2) the feeling that comes about when things don't go one's way (Discontentment), 3) the feeling that one is never satisfied (Hunger and Thirst), 4) intense feelings of attachment (Obsession), 5) feelings of apathy and losing motivation (Sloth), 6) the feeling of inferiority and being afraid (Fear), 7) the feeling of distrust (Doubt), 8) the feeling of obstinacy

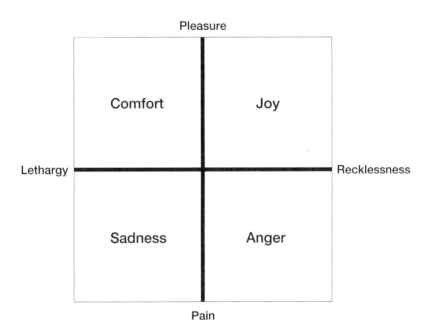

Chart 6 : Joy, Anger, Sadness, and Comfort and the Soul Compass

(Stubbornness).

Although the Buddhist legend holds that these feelings were sent to give trouble to the Buddha in his last stages of enlightenment, they might more broadly be thought of as aspects of human bewilderment. If we categorize these eight feelings into the chart featuring the **four personality types** (see Chart 7), they could be divided as follows:

Pain-Recklessness (Resentful Victim Type): Discontentment, Stubbornness, Doubt

Pleasure-Recklessness (Over-Confident Type): Greed, Hunger and Thirst, Obsession

Pain-Lethargy (Self-Depreciating Type): Fear

Pleasure-Lethargy (Self-Satisfied Type): Sloth

In this Buddhist analysis of human emotion, we can see that more careful consideration was given to emotions in the **Recklessness** zone. This can probably be attributed to the historical background of the Buddha's age in which fighting among clans and more **Recklessness** type of reactions to the world's events could be seen. It is therefore not surprising that more attention would be paid to emotions associated with such trends. Needless to say, the social and historical contexts of these types of analyses of human emotions must be taken into account as we seek to understand various approaches to this human quest to understand the human mind.

Another such historical context is early medieval China, when the founder of the T'ien-T'ai Buddhist tradition, Chih-i (538-597), systematized Buddhist sutras and commentaries from India. One of the texts was a meditation manual, *The T'ien-T'ai Short Text on Stopping-and-Seeing Meditation*, which described five "hindrances" to attaining enlightenment. These five hindrances thus correspond to the veil which covers the **true self**. These five obstacles to human enlightenment are: Greed, Anger, Doubt, Confusion, and Sloth.

In traditional Buddhism, it was said that humans were afflicted with "three poisons" (Greed, Anger, Ignorance) that clouded their ability to act with wisdom and compassion. The three negative qualities that poison the mind are reflected in the five hindrances with Greed and Anger as part of the list and Ignorance being broken down further into Doubt and Sloth, while Confusion was considered a result of the mixing of the three poisons. It was claimed in the meditation manual that

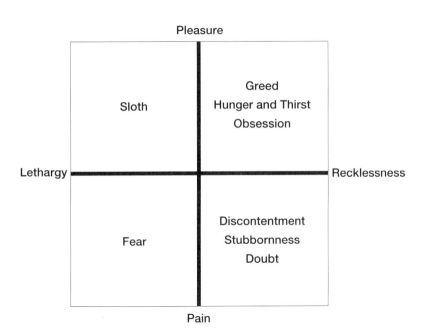

Chart 7 : The Eight Armies (Feelings) and the Soul Compass

if one removed these five hindrances, one could remove all the obstacles to enlightenment.

If we put aside Confusion (which is a composite emotion), we can find that this ancient Buddhist categorization of negative emotions also corresponds to our **soul compass** chart (see Chart 8). For example, Greed corresponds to the **Pleasure-Recklessness** zone and is a part of the **Over-Confident** personality type. In Buddhist texts, it is often said that greed is characterized by immense longing for something, a fear of losing it once one has it, and resentment once one has lost it.

Anger lies in the **Pain-Recklessness** zone as a characteristic of the **Resentful Victim** personality type. In a classical Buddhist text, a dialogue between the Buddha and a heavenly deity helps us understand the nature of anger. The deity asks the Buddha, "What do I need to kill to achieve equanimity? What do I need to kill to become free from sadness?" Sensing the extreme anger lodged within the deity and the tendency to find the cause of sadness outside himself, the Buddha answered, "If you kill Anger, you will achieve equanimity and be free from sadness. Anger is the root poison that destroys good." This exchange carries with it a deep teaching. It tells us that though we may ordinarily think that to protect ourselves we need to get angry at other people, in fact, the enemy is within not without. To achieve true equanimity and freedom from sadness, instead of looking outside, one needs to protect oneself and fight the enemy within, namely, anger.

Doubt lies in the **Pain-Lethargy** zone and is characteristic of the **Self-Depreciating** personality type. In Buddhism, doubt is said to be the factor that prevents decision making and looking deeply into the nature of things. Born of Ignorance, doubt is the most evil of all evils. This is because doubt is really self-doubt and in Buddhism, it is thought that we all possess Buddha-nature, or the potential seeds to become a Buddha. Thus to doubt oneself is to doubt one's ability to become a Buddha or by **Self-Depreciating**, doubt one's ability to walk the Buddhist path.

Finally, Sloth can be found in the **Pleasure-Lethargy** zone characterizing the **Self-Satisfied** personality type. A Buddhist teacher once cautioned a disciple who was slothful and always falling asleep that such daydreaming is like being in a room with a poisonous snake. Since sloth is like a great darkness in which one's consciousness and

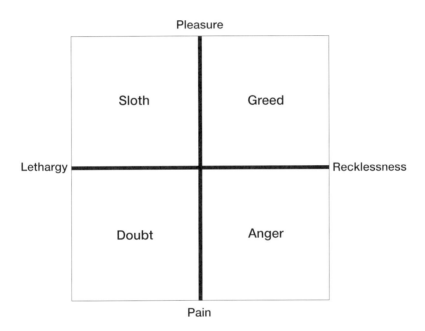

Chart 8 : The Five Hindrances and the Soul Compass

ability to be aware of one's acts and their consequences on others are taken away, it was a very dangerous thing.

Whether it is with these five hindrances or the other traditional classifications of human emotions (such as the Japanese joy, anger, sadness, and comfort classification or the early Buddhist eight "armies"), we have been able to see how they correspond to the **soul compass**. With the **Pleasure-Pain Axis** and the **Recklessness-Lethargy Axis** providing a framework for the four zones of the **soul compass**, we can notice how various ways **to look within ourselves** developed by religious leaders over the centuries fit into our new system. With this new system for the current age, we can more readily enter into the practice of looking within and studying ourselves.

The Wisdom of the Soul Compass II : The Power to Connect Our Inner Selves and the Outer World

The Soul Compass Which Is Able to Penetrate Reality

To be aware of the **four personality types** we discussed above is essential to the practice of looking within ourselves. But the **soul compass** is also essential to the practice of connecting our inner selves and the outer world. This is crucial because reality as such is constructed through an interaction of the inner and outer worlds. The **soul compass** allows us to see what we usually aren't aware of, that is, how our **mind-and-form unit** is related to the nature of our minds and to the reality of the outer world. To understand the principles that govern this interaction and the complexity of this reality helps us to deal with and transcend the negative realities that are presented to us.

The Four Blades That Turn Chaos into Negative Realities

The **four personality types** discussed above, when seen more dynamically as they appear in the world, are hurtful factors that cut like blades into the **chaos** (Figure 14). We might recall that **chaos** includes within itself both light and darkness. What the **four blades** do is to cut into chaos in such a way as to destroy the light and turn everything toward the negative.

These **four blades** destroy reality not only on an individual level, but in larger social units including national and transnational levels. In

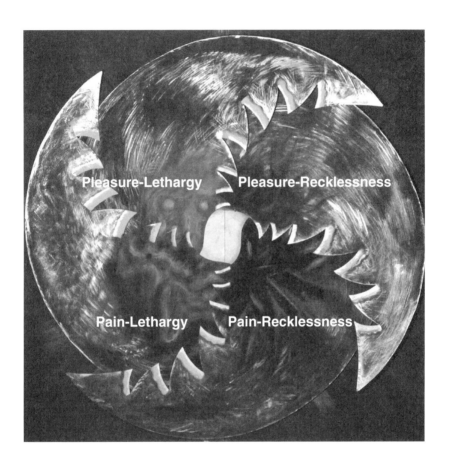

Figure 14 : The Four Blades

the course of human history there have been individuals who stood up to these blades. The rise and fall of nations and empires has been determined by how individuals dealt with the movement of these **four blades** in history.

Great empires, such as Sung China or the Roman Empire, rose and fell because of how individuals dealt with the **four blades**. Chinese emperors, for instance, tending toward one or the other type of personalities, acted in ways that undermined their authority and moved the country toward ever increasing anxiety and violence, ultimately leading to the fall of this great empire. In the case of the Roman Empire, it is well known that in its last days, the ever-increasing luxurious life style of its elite (**Pleasure-Lethargy**) led to its downfall.

In modern German history, we can also see the workings of the **four blades**. After losing World War I, many Germans were highly discontent (**Pain-Recklessness**) and playing on these feelings emerged Adolf Hitler (1889-1945). Heightening these feelings of **Pain-Recklessness** to his own political benefit, he recklessly put forth from this situation a new movement of Aryan superiority that, as is well known, ended in the genocide of millions of Jews and others.

In Japanese history, a similar rise and fall can be seen in the Warring States period. Just before this 100-year period of tremendous warfare across Japan among various feudal lords, power was held by the shogun, Ashikaga Yoshimasa (1436-90). His reign as the shogun was marked by **Pain-Lethargy** and **Pleasure-Lethargy**. The country was in a state of degeneration as harvests failed several years in a row, provoking peasant unrest and an inability of the shogunate to do anything about it. While the peasants were in pain, the shogun and his retinue were enjoying a pleasurable, lavish life. Building lavish palaces and temples and putting on sumptuous poetry parties, trying to emulate the "golden age" of his predecessors, Yoshimasa had no qualms about placing a huge financial burden on the peasantry. While Yoshimasa managed to create a magnificent cultural renaissance with his generous patronage of artists and craftsmen, he also laid the groundwork for the collapse of the shogunate and the degeneration into war. This situation of lavish spending by the shogunate and the imposition of great hardships on the peasantry, among other factors, sparked a divide between the shogunate and the emperor Go-Hanazono which led to the so-called Ohnin War and the beginnings of decades of warfare.

This warfare involved the washing of blood with blood as successive feudal lords battled for supremacy. In the end, the feudal lord Oda Nobunaga (1534-82) managed to conquer all others and unify the country under his control. He created a new order after going on a rampage of violence against any and all who stood in his way. His pleasure in victory propelled even further conflicts until his goal to unify the country was attained (**Pleasure-Recklessness**).

As can be seen in the above examples, the principle of the rise and fall of empires and nations can be found across the ages and continents. This principle is even true today as we look at modern-day Japan. Though it is clear that, after the war, Japan managed to rebuild itself into one of the most powerful economic powers (**Pleasure-Recklessness**) from extreme poverty and suffering (**Pain**), the quick transition to prosperity has inevitably started to shift toward a lackadaisical attitude about life. People have become seemingly content materially but have started to question their pleasure individually and as a nation. As can be seen in the prolonged economic recession or the rise in juvenile crimes, Japan will cycle into pain, both reckless and lethargic.

The Four False Selves and the Four Blades

The Four False Selves: Their Mistaken Convictions and the Reality Created from Them

Let us further examine the **four personality types** in their negative representations—the four false selves—by understanding the **mistaken convictions** that lie in their background. These convictions lie at the root of the false selves, which, when put in motion in the world, turn into the **four blades**. The interaction of the **four blades** with the world, then, goes on to create our **mind-and-form units** (Chart 9). Therefore to stop these blades from acting on us and the world in this way, we must look back on the **mistaken convictions** which lie in its backdrop (Charts 10-11).

The Four False Selves	The Four Zones	The Four Blades	The Mistaken Convictions	The Reality That Is Created	The Formula for Losing
Over-Confident Type	Pleasure-Recklessness	Pleasure-Recklessness Blade	Spiritual Irrelevance	Exploitation	Contempt
Resentful Victim Type	Pain-Recklessness	Pain-Recklessness Blade	Mistrust of Others	Destruction	Violence
Self-Depreciating Type	Pain-Lethargy	Pain-Lethargy Blade	Mistrust of Oneself	Debilitation	Giving Up
Self-Satisfied Type	Pleasure-Lethargy	Pleasure-Lethargy Blade	Reality Irrelevance	Conformity	Neglect

Chart 9 : The Mind-and-Form Unit of the False Self

Over-Confident Type（Pleasure-Recklessness）:
Spiritual Irrelevance

Resentful Victim Type（Pain-Recklessness）:
Mistrust of Others

Self-Depreciating Type（Pain-Lethargy）:
Mistrust of Oneself

Self-Satisfied Type（Pleasure-Lethargy）:
Reality Irrelevance

Chart 10 : The Mistaken Convictions of the Four False Selves

Over-Confident Type（Pleasure-Recklessness）:
Exploitation

Resentful Victim Type（Pain-Recklessness）:
Destruction

Self-Depreciating Type（Pain-Lethargy）:
Debilitation

Self-Satisfied Type（Pleasure-Lethargy）:
Conformity

Chart 11 : The Reality That Is Created by the Four Blades

Over-Confident Type : An Alchemist Who Believes He Can Do Anything (Exploitation)

The mistaken conviction of the **Over-Confident** type is the idea that if everything is going smoothly, then, spiritual matters are irrelevant. The orientation of this personality toward **Pleasure-Recklessness** means that rather than inner meaning, the person is oriented toward external results (**spiritual irrelevance**). Trying to generate a better phenomenal reality, his emphasis is on materialism.

Because of an over-confidence in his ability, this result-oriented personality believes that it's acceptable to be a little dishonest as long as things go his way. This demonstrates the lack of attention given to moral and spiritual matters. The over-emphasis on material reality means that true reality slips further and further away so that in the end, reality is constructed to always fit his schema and is constantly skewed. Changing and concocting a delusional reality like an alchemist, this type of personality ultimately leads himself down the path of self-destruction.

The self-righteous attitude of this type of person thus creates a reality which exploits others. What this means is that when confronted with the neutral, chaotic reality, the tendency is to unravel it for his own self-created reality. This unraveling often means that reality is skewed in such a way that it hurts and exploits others, though ultimately, this deformed reality comes back to haunt and hurt the person himself.

Of course, this type of exploitative reality occurs not just on an individual level, but on a broader basis. The numerous environmental issues we face today—the destruction of the ozone layer, the increase of carbon dioxide, acid rain, global warming, the depletion of natural resources—have all been caused by the exploitative approach to the world. While we have been trying to gain the most convenient life style and create a reality that suits only the human species, the natural world has paid a huge price. But in the end, we humans are now having to pay a huge price as the skewing of reality has come full circle to haunt us.

This exploitative attitude toward reality is not limited to the natural world, but we can see the exact same pattern in human society. For example, the creation of the self-indulgent bubble economy in Japan during the late 1980s, which witnessed the buying sprees of expensive

Western art and properties overseas, land and stock speculation, ended up exploiting regular people. When the companies, which engaged in such practices faced the burst of the bubble, the resultant 70 trillion yen debt had to be resolved through public taxpayers' money thus exploiting and hurting the vast majority of people who had nothing to do with the creation of such a reality. This massive miscalculation based on a delusional vision of never-ending growth affected not only the taxpayers, but the Japanese economy and even the world economy as a whole.

Resentful Victim Type : A Philosopher Who Believes the World Is Evil (Destruction)

The mistaken conviction of the **Resentful Victim** type is that the reason things don't go well is the fault of others, situations, or fate. This personality type, based on **Pain-Recklessness**, believes that his or her pain is caused by unfairness in the world and therefore there is a negative generation of **mistrust of others**. Always thinking that the world is unfair, this type is like a philosopher constantly musing that the world is fundamentally evil. This conviction is continually strengthened by noting the unfairness of the world when people treat him harshly and even when kindness is offered by others, always thinking that there must be an evil catch to it.

Taking on the whole world as the "enemy," when things go wrong, such a person always blames the "other," never bothering to look within himself. Always thinking of himself as the victim, there is a mistaken conviction that the best way to protect himself and live in this world is to take revenge when hurt or even to attack before he is attacked. In this way, even when there is no real threat, this personality type's **mind-and-form unit** makes up threats and destroys things of value.

Although the 20th century has been characterized as the century of scientific and technological advances, it was also the century which witnessed the great destruction and loss of human life. It is said that between the two world wars, 30 million people perished. Even at the end of the 20th century, just in the past few years, we have seen this cycle of destruction in the form of wars, terrorism, and ethnic conflicts continue in places as far apart as Chechnya, Northern Ireland, and Israel.

This type of wanton destruction is not carried out by any other species than the human species. We have engaged in these cycles of destruction because of the working of the **Resentful Victim** type unable to contain this negative orientation toward violence.

Self-Depreciating Type : A Scientist Who Searches for Evidence of Impossibility (Debilitation)
The mistaken conviction of the **Self-Depreciating** type is that however hard one might wish or will something to happen, his inner intentions have no effect on the world. This **mistrust of oneself** of the **Self-Depreciating** personality is based on a disbelief in the power of human inner potential that leads to **Pain-Lethargy**.

Such a person is like a scientist constantly searching for evidence of impossibility. Believing that the human is unable to change reality in the slightest, this personality always sets up the hypotheses of "Such a thing is impossible" or "It can't be changed" and then, works furiously to find evidence supporting these hypotheses to end up with the conclusion that it is impossible to affect the world.

Accumulating evidence after evidence to support these hypotheses, the hypotheses become fact for the **Self-Depreciating** type. This personality suffers from this inability to change the world and through this constant drumroll of "Such a thing is impossible," he kills all creativity. Although chaotic reality has potential and though it is hard to draw out this potential for creative and imaginative things, the **Self-Depreciating** type becomes lethargic, turning into a person totally incapable of turning reality toward the positive.

Thus, as he gives up on influencing the course of events in the world, the reality of debilitation is all that is left. This kind of "giving up" on the world or a sense of debilitation can be found on a societal level as well. In recent years in Japan, there has been a noticeable increase in the use of drugs among young people. Although they might give various reasons for taking drugs—as a tool for dieting, for studying, or just for the pleasure of getting high—there is a deep sense of nihilism and giving up about the whole phenomena. In all of our major cities, this sense of nihilism about community building, where we don't seem to even know our neighbors anymore, seems rampant. This negative sensibility of giving up on the world is characteristic of the reality of debilitation.

Self-Satisfied Type : An Indifferent Person Who Lives Light-Heartedly (Conformity)

The mistaken conviction of the **Self-Satisfied** type is that if he feels fine, however troubled the reality, it doesn't matter. In contrast to the **Over-Confident** type who favors material reality over the inner reality, for the Self-Satisfied, external reality is irrelevant as long as his or her feelings are fine (**reality irrelevance**). This personality type, who is moved by **Pleasure-Lethargy**, is apathetic to and light-hearted about the world, not caring about its troubles and hardships. Such a person is aloof and appears genteel, focusing on self-satisfaction that looks deceptively like caring about inner spirituality.

This approach to life is what some have termed "positive thinking" in which the person simply gets stuck on positive aspects and ignores the negative. We should note here that the approach I am advocating is not so simple in that the **Grand Challenge** requires us to carefully accept and understand both the positive and negative. This is because such positive thinking is based on a false hope. Real hope for transforming ourselves and the world comes only after truly seeing ourselves, both the good and the bad, and regretting the negative aspects of ourselves. This regret is what propels us into a new life for the first time. The **Self-Satisfied** type ends up apathetically living each day and he is unable to distinguish between the positive and negative aspects of **chaos**, choosing to ignore half the equation and holding onto a half-hearted false hope. To live truly one must be able to distinguish the positive and negative aspects of reality and prevent the negative while encouraging the positive.

The mind-and-form unit of the Self-Satisfied type poses serious problems especially in countries like Japan where prosperity has proceeded so far and so rapidly. Unable to think of anything that doesn't affect one's immediate wants and concerns, this self-centered ignorance about one's fortunate position to live in such prosperity builds arrogance and limitations on one's sense of responsibility to the world.

This type of complacency about the world is reflected in the sense of conformity that characterizes contemporary Japanese society. According to the annual survey conducted by the Prime Minister's

Office on Japanese life styles, approximately 90% of Japanese think that they are middle class and 60% think that their lives are "normal." The "conformist" tendency to think that the current situation is acceptable by most Japanese should be a warning about Japan's future. The leading Japanese economic newspaper, the Nihon Keizai Shimbun, has warned that the current Japanese economic and social climate is similar to Victorian England where most people were swallowed up in a dreamlike stupor about the greatness of their country and their future. But this lackadaisical attitude ultimately led to the overtaking of Britain by the United States and Germany within the space of 30 years in steel production and in other fields. Other institute and government reports, such as those commissioned by the United States government and Shell Oil Group, have also pointed out the slow pace of Japanese economic and policy-level restructuring and reforms in a time when speed counts the most. The conformity and complacent nature of Japanese today, born from the **Self-Satisfied** personality, will surely lead to Japan's downfall.

Numerous problems in the world today are rooted in the **exploitation**, **destruction**, **debilitation**, and **conformity** that are created by the **four personality types**.

The Formula for Winning and Losing

The Law of Disintegration and the Law of Uncontrollability

We have now discussed the variables that go into the reasons why we tend to develop **mind-and-form units** or attitudes that turn **chaos**, which naturally has both positive and negative potentials, toward the negative. In addition to the construction of our inner psyche, however, there is also something in the outer world that also orients **chaos** to turn negative. This is **the law of disintegration** and **the law of uncontrollability**. Unless we understand these strict laws of the universe, we will neither be able to understand our **mind-and-form units** nor shift **chaos** toward the light.

The law of disintegration means that all things and events eventually self-destruct or cease to exist. All things, without exception, follow this law. Things that exist disintegrate and everything that lives eventually dies. For example, if we think of biology, all living beings, however full of vitality, at some point age and come to an end. The cells of the body, which give order to all living creatures, degenerate as the body grows old and ultimately waste away as the body disintegrates. In terms of physics, the law of entropy, the second law of thermodynamics, also suggests a similar concept: that the entropy of an object or being increases with time. This means that matter and energy always move from order to disorder, available energy to unavailable energy, and usability to uselessness.

This law is also at work within the human soul as well. Our relationships and friendships, which we may have thought of as secure and everlasting, quite often come to an end. Couples that started out deeply in love with each other and pledging to be life partners often end up resenting each other or splitting in divorce. People also lose meaning and purpose in life that they may have once had. And all this is because of **the law of disintegration** which governs our world.

The structure of a human life bestowed to us in this world—birth, old age, illness, and death—also reflects **the law of disintegration**, and in addition, exemplifies **the law of uncontrollability**. Uncontrollability is based on the fact that things don't always go the way one wants. Nobody wants to grow old or die, but it is the nature of the world. Loved ones pass away while we have to be around people we don't particularly like. Our deep greed that goes against the processes of the world laments the fact that things don't go according to how we would like it. This disappointment with the world often leads us to losing our purpose and mission in life, a type of uncontrollability.

Because of **the law of disintegration** and **the law of uncontrollability**, in addition to the **four personality types** we discussed above, **chaos**, though neutral, is not equally balanced between the negative and positive. Though it has the potential to turn negative or positive, it is weighted far more heavily on the negative side. And once **chaos** takes form, it cannot return to the formless state again, which means that negativity once released is not reversible. Time and time again, we humans seem to turn things toward the negative throughout history in a repetitious cycle because of the strong pull of the inner (the **four personality types** and **four blades**) and outer structures (**the law of disintegration** and **the law of uncontrollability**) of the world. Because of the odds of turning negative, if we are to rise to the Grand Challenge of turning ourselves and the world toward the positive, we must confront these principles and laws both within ourselves and in the world. With wisdom and a strong will, we must start walking on the path that leads toward the light.

The Formula for Losing

Although we have just mentioned that we need to confront the **four blades**, we should not think that we can use them to overcome **the law of disintegration** and **the law of uncontrollability**. Indeed, if we imagine we can somehow play with the rules of the world and win, we are sadly mistaken. Getting entangled with the **four blades** to change either ourselves or the world is a sure **formula for losing**.

Losing by Contempt : Over-Confident Type (Pleasure-Recklessness)

The **Over-Confident** type, because of over-confidence in their own abilities, tends to think that they can control the world. They are happy as long as everything is going well materially neglecting their inner selves. The emphasis on material pleasure means that such people are result-oriented and try to shape the world according to their vision of what it should be (**spiritual irrelevance**).

Under **the law of disintegration, chaos** cannot be easily controlled or changed as one desires. But **Over-Confident** types believe that they can alter this iron-clad **law of disintegration**. This demonstrates a highly arrogant contempt for the laws of the world. This contempt leads such types to embark on courses of action that take on the world's most basic laws, but end up losing to those laws, causing pain not only for themselves but for everyone else they happen to involve in their endeavors. People involved in the seemingly ceaseless financial scandals in Japan, or more broadly speaking, people involved in the creation of the atomic bomb or major environmental destruction exemplify the type of people who think that they can control the world. But as we well know, such actions against nature have ended out of control and with the pains of many.

Losing by Violence : Resentful Victim Type (Pain-Recklessness)

The **Resentful Victim** type, instead of recognizing the natural law of disintegration, tends to be overcome with feelings of unfairness about

Over-Confident Type (Pleasure-Recklessness) :
Contempt

Resentful Victim Type (Pain-Recklessness) :
Violence

Self-Depreciating Type (Pain-Lethargy) :
Giving Up

Self-Satisfied Type (Pleasure-Lethargy) :
Neglect

Chart 12 : The Formula for Losing with the Four Blades

the world. Unable to trust others, such types generate angry and violent responses to the conditions of the world (**mistrust of others**). Even though creating things in this world is time-consuming and difficult, the **Resentful Victim** type has no problem destroying such creations, even if they are of their own making.

The violence that dwells within such persons at times proceeds to provoke the latent violence in others. War, for instance, is the expression of violence begetting violence in which each side feels victimized and a need for revenge. This cycle, therefore, ends up hastening and multiplying the impact of **the law of disintegration** and **the law of uncontrollability**.

Losing by Giving Up : Self-Depreciating Type (Pain-Lethargy)

The **Self-Depreciating** type, when faced with the very same **law of disintegration** and **the law of uncontrollability**, ends up giving up on the world. Whether it's a bankruptcy of their company or the worsening of an illness, when things start to disintegrate, for such people, it quickly moves from bad to worse in a domino effect. Burdened with a nihilistic worldview, the **Self-Depreciating** person loses by giving up (**mistrust of oneself**). Giving up becomes the only answer for such people because to really overcome such situations, under **the law of disintegration** and **the law of uncontrollability**, requires a strong sense of love, will, and perseverance, which is lacking in this type.

Losing by Neglect : Self-Satisfied Type (Pleasure-Lethargy)

The **Self-Satisfied** type, as discussed above, tends to ignore the realities of the world and lives in a bubble of self-contentment (**Pleasure-Lethargy** zone). However, when this type faces **the law of disintegration**, it comes as a complete shock when their bubble bursts due to the sharpness of the reality of disintegration. Such people tend to live in a fantasy world oblivious to the actual world (**reality irrelevance**), always moving toward a comfort-zone away from the harshness of reality. However, the further removed from reality they are, the harder it hits when the fantasy is dispelled. And yet when such harsh realities are shown, such people have no ability to take this as a lesson about their worldview, but it simply becomes a brief setback for them before they go on their self-satisfied way, avoiding pain and neglecting reality as such.

The Formula for Winning : The Mind-and-Form Unit of the True Self

As we have seen, the **four blades** can only lead to formulas for losing against the laws of the world. But there is a source for transcending the laws of the world located deep within ourselves: the **true self** which lies at the center of our souls. How we access the **true self** is the key to the formulas for winning against **the law of disintegration** and **the law of uncontrollability**.

Trust of Oneself (Conviction)

In the **true self**, one has a deep-seated conviction about the way things ought to be. This is qualitatively vastly different from the arrogant self-confidence of the **Over-Confident**. Instead of a confidence that comes from comparing oneself with others and thinking that one is better, true conviction comes from a place beyond comparison and is therefore an absolute, rather than a relative, trust in oneself. This **true self** therefore has inner conviction and finds joy in complete resonance with the spirit of the universe.

Trust of Others (Faith)

The **true self**, in addition to an authentic trust in oneself, also embodies a true trust of and faith in others. While the **Self-Satisfied** type may have an optimistic and unfounded faith in others, the true self's faith in others is based on an accurate assessment of the true nature of things. This faith in the world is also absolute. Even though the world is full of conflict, injustice, and inequality, the true self's faith in the world and others, while acknowledging these realities, reaches beyond them.

Importance of the Spirit (Awe)

The **true self** also deeply understands the importance of the human spirit or the inner world for it recognizes the broken nature of the world when the spirit is cut off from the world. In contrast to the **Over-Confident** type's sense of contempt, it faces the world with awe. And yet this awe is not the fear of the world embodied by the **Self-**

Trust of Oneself（Conviction）

Trust of Others（Faith）

Importance of the Spirit（Awe）

Importance of Reality（Responsibility）

Chart 13 : The Mind-and-Form Unit of the True Self

Depreciating type, but is an awe born of the conviction that one can entrust oneself to a power greater and more awesome than oneself and yet put down one's own roots.

Importance of Reality (Responsibility)

The **true self** recognizes the reality of **the law of disintegration** and **the law of uncontrollability**, but instead of feeling victimized and unfair about the nature of the world, the **true self** understands his or her place within it. In other words, while one lives in a world of disintegration and uncontrollability, the true self is able to stand up as a responsible member of the world community to eke out a proper way to live within it. If there is a single being in the universe that is suffering, the **true self** suffers along with him.

We must let go of the **four blades** and our false selves to form a new **mind-and-form unit** based on our true selves from the depths of our souls. When we access and free our true selves from the bonds of the **false self**, we are able to resonate with the **six forces** of the universe we discussed in Chapter 1. When we are able to accomplish this, we are able to undertake the **Grand Challenge** of **resonating with the universe** and transforming **chaos** to light. Below are the records of some people who managed to make this transformation.

Records of the Grand Challenge

A Record of an Individual's Grand Challenge IV

Shoichi Tsumura was age 56 when he passed away last year. He was the proprietor of a food-services company in Hokkaido, the northernmost island of Japan. The crisis that proved to be his transformative experience was an incident one day when some of the school lunches which his company provided to 1,600 children at the local schools were reported to have had a strange taste. Fearing food poisoning, the local school council (which together with many other organizations had approved the contract for this service) contacted all the schools to stop serving Mr. Tsumura's products for lunch. Furthermore, other retailers that Mr. Tsumura's company serviced were also contacted to warn them about the possibility of defective food. Since the calls were made right at lunchtime, it caused a great commotion.

Especially since the mass media had recently reported on outbreaks of *E. coli* food poisoning, the local papers took up this incident on their front pages. What followed was a huge crisis (**chaos**) for Mr. Tsumura's company as the local school council, the PTA, the school president, and the local food services council all got involved.

Mr. Tsumura had, from a young age, two personality types (**Over-Confident** and **Resentful Victim**). Because of his over-confidence, he would most likely have understood this incident as having been caused by external factors and would have been the last person to look within himself to explain the crisis. Further because of his feelings as a **Resentful Victim**, he would have thought it unfair that something like this happened. He would probably have immediately thought to call a lawyer and also tried to search for the culprit (whether it be the employee that managed that food sample or his or her immediate supervisor, or basically anyone but himself).

If he had, in fact, gone ahead with such steps, we can imagine the following type of scenario. His over-reaction by retaining a lawyer, for example, may have made his clients reluctant to seek his company services in the future even if he managed to win the lawsuit. Or his hunting down of a culprit in the company may have caused multiple repercussions such as employees fearing their boss. This, in turn, may have led to a lack of innovation, as employees all bunkered down to avoid being the next causality. The lack of innovation in a food service company would have also led to the downfall of the firm. These thoughts, apparently, ran through Mr. Tsumura's mind momentarily when he was faced with this crisis.

Mr. Tsumura grew up in a fisherman's home, but his father died when he was still young. His mother, who had to struggle raising childen on her own and with problems like how to negotiate the family finances with members of the extended family, gave Mr. Tsumura a harsh view of reality. She told him not to trust others and to always be on top. He became the class bully and grew up thinking that if he worked hard he would make it in the world. Ignoring inner, spiritual world, he was result-oriented and focused on the material world (**Over-Confident**). In addition, because of the loss of his father at a young age, he also felt that the world was against him and he was a victim (**Resentful Victim**).

Although he had grown up in such a way, Mr. Tsumura had practiced the concepts of the Grand Challenge and instead of going down the road that would have been natural, he told himself to stop and look deeply into this situation to understand why he was feeling anger and like a victim.

Thus, instead of the negative path, he decided to turn toward his **true self**. His **true self** had the conviction that there must be a way to resolve this situation without resorting to anger or victimhood. Indeed, he decided to immediately pay a visit to the local school council and all the others involved in the incident, taking the unprecedented step of saying, "Whatever the fallout of this incident, the responsibility is all mine." With this attitude of self-responsibility, others began a swift investigation into the suspected food source and cooperated with him fully. The results were an all-clear on the food and not a single child got ill. The whole incident blew over in two days and he even received an apology from the local school council head that their reaction was overblown.

This incident had further repercussions within his company as the employees banded behind their president who had covered for all of them. His actions turned a negative into a positive and the resultant company cohesiveness was simply a by-product of his new **mind-and-form unit**. His attitude also impressed the local school council to the extent that he was offered a contract to work together to serve lunches to children using Hokkaido produce. Instead of a very probable negative course of events, his new **mind-and-form unit** allowed him to block the negative, increase the positive, and ultimately bring greater possibilities for his company. This is the power of turning to the **true self** when confronted with **chaos**.

A Record of an Individual's Grand Challenge V

Takeshi Mishima, age 51, is the owner of a restaurant chain in western Japan. He grew up with a very strong victim's personality which erupted in violence to those around him. It was only when he realized the effects of his actions on those around him that he began to regret this orientation of hurting others and tried to find a different path. After a long period of self-reflection, he managed to create many opportunities to turn toward the light-filled positive direction in both his work and family contexts.

One of the incidents that set him off to search for a new direction was when he learned that his wife was affected with stress-caused hair loss and anorexia. At the time, his family life was in dire straits as he barely communicated with his wife in a joyless marriage and further-more, his son was afflicted with a serious kidney disease. The situation at work was not any better as his relationships with his employees were at an all-time low and he found that he had reached the limit of his chain-restaurant expansion. However, throughout this difficult period, Mr. Mishima never sought out causes of this situation within himself, always looking to external factors.

His strong **Resentful Victim** personality reflected here began when he was a young boy of eight. Mr. Mishima had been born in a fairly poor farming family and during the busiest time of the farming season, his mother promised the young boy that if he worked hard to help with the harvest, she would buy him a bicycle. Only thinking about how great it would be to have a bicycle, Mr. Mishima worked extremely hard to help out with the harvest. However, when the season came to an end and he went to his mother for the bicycle, she told him that she had never made such a promise. From this time on, he told himself never to trust anyone again as he wallowed in sadness and anger.

For many children, a parent is everything and to have been betrayed in such a way causes deep wounds. From that time on, Mr. Mishima "mistrusted others" and this mistrust toward the world at large grew every time a similar incident occurred. His resultant anger toward the world continued into his adult life as he pressed his wife to be a perfect wife and mother to his children who would never ever betray him or his children. His pressuring her in this way caused great stress for his wife. His badgering also occurred at the workplace mak-ing everyone fearful of him and unable to communicate with him in a pleasant way.

It was around this time that Mr. Mishima started to join the TL Seminars (Total Life Human Principles Seminars), which form the foundations of the Grand Challenge. His learning of some of the tools to understand his personality helped him recognize a very important lesson in an incident a few days after a seminar. That day, his wife called him during a business meeting to ask him about a tax-related matter. He cut her off the phone almost immediately, shouting, "Taxes are not my area, you're supposed to be in charge of our finances. Figure it out yourself!" It was then that he realized that his wife had called him about the taxes because she had simply been afraid of not doing them right and had called to get his approval. He became aware that his response to her was a form of condemnation and that because of his repeated condemnations of her, she had become overly fearful of failure and unable to make her own decisions. Thus, he came to understand that the reason his wife was the way she was derived from his hurtful behavior toward her. He could not contain his feelings of great remorse toward how he had treated her over the years.

His turn toward his **true self** allowed him to integrate his inner self and the outer world again. He was able to improve communications with his family. Everyone noticed how much better his wife looked recently. His employees also noticed a much happier Mr. Mishima and found they could communicate with him better. The turn toward the light-filled positive reality also appeared in the form of a better business environment which meant an increase in the number of his restaurants. Mr. Mishima now lives each day as a wonderful father, husband, and mentor for his employees as he was able to embark on this transformative Grand Challenge.

A Record of an Individual's Grand Challenge VI

Tomoko Koriyama, age 43, is currently a high school teacher in Chiba Prefecture. She is trying to be a teacher that not only covers the curriculum, but tries to nurture each of her students' spiritual life as well. However, things were not always like this.

Not all that long ago, Ms. Koriyama felt that she did not fit in anywhere she went. She had a strong mistrust of herself and a complete lack of confidence in her abilities. Thus, she constantly thought that other people looked down on her or were opposed to her. This bred a strong personality type which mistrusted others.

What this meant at school was that if there were antagonistic students in her classroom, she would easily lose her confidence as a teacher and worry about how her colleagues would view her inability to handle the students. Ultimately, as she tried to deal with such situations, she fell into a controlling relationship with her students. But trying to control such rebellious students always backfired and the students' hearts drifted further and further away from her. These situations compounded with each other to create increasingly strong patterns of mistrust in herself as well as in others.

She thus resigned herself to the fact that she could not do anything about such students and quickly blamed external factors, such as the students' families for causing such a situation. That Ms. Koriyama had such deeply ingrained **Pain-Lethargy** had its origins in her childhood.

Ms. Koriyama had a major accident when she was just one and a half years old, falling from a second-story veranda. Resulting from the fall, two years later she developed a hip joint disorder. She was told that she would have walking problems throughout her life. Fortunately, she was able to recover and walk in a few years, but she initially had to spend most of her days at home with a cast upon being released from the hospital, rather than playing with her friends. All seemed fine until the sixth grade, when one evening she began having convulsive seizures and lost consciousness. She was taken to a hospital where she was told that something in her brain had been damaged and that she had had an epileptic fit. She was totally taken aback when she looked up her condition in a medical dictionary and found that it could lead to epileptic dementia. She started to withdraw further and further into herself, timidly avoiding contact with others.

She constantly wondered why so many things had been taken away from her childhood. Throughout junior and senior high school, she had not been able to open up to other people about this hurt within herself and so when it came time for her to choose a career path, she thought she would try to be a school teacher, who would be able to open up to her students. However, as we noted, far from being able to open up to her students, she was repelled by them.

It was around then that Ms. Koriyama began to study the Truth. Using the **soul compass**, she began to understand the roots of her personality type and deeply regretted that she kept on pushing students away. In the process of healing her own spirit, she began to also notice a change in the way she related to her students. For example, right around that time, a troubled student who had to repeat the school year because he was so frequently absent, enrolled in Ms. Koriyama's homeroom. He came to school infrequently and when he did, he seemed to never talk with anyone or if he did, angry words seemed all that would come out. In the past, Ms. Koriyama would probably have tried to sweep the problem student under the rug and only cared about what her colleagues thought about her. And indeed, when she had to confront this student, he made her lose her confidence completely.

But because she had begun her spiritual journey and come to understand why her personality type made her react in this way, she boldly set out on a different course of action, one without excuses. She constantly asked herself what she could do with what abilities she had. She began to relate to the troubled student as a human being, one-on-one, rather than from a position of superiority. Amazingly, the student began slowly opening up to her and over time, the student came out of his shell. This transformation encouraged the student's parents to come to Ms. Koriyama to let her know how grateful they were and how they had not realized their son's potential. Although the student wasn't ultimately able to fulfill the requirements to graduate that year, he made the round of all his teachers to personally thank them for their help.

When she decided to trust in the student by opening up to him, that leap of faith was rewarded with his opening up to her. Even the boy's parents were able to open up and trust again. Through this incident, Ms. Koriyama was able to have the conviction that if she engaged in the world fully, it would definitely respond to her. She also recognized just how much her **Pain-Lethargy** had blinded her to reality and skewed her sense of the nature of the world. While she had previously thought that she had been given an awful life with so much hurt, she came to realize that hers was indeed a life blessed with loving parents and others who had looked after her. Her sense of gratitude toward the world was boundless. This gratitude has become the basis of her new life as an educator, responsible for the nurturing of those who will grow up in the 21st century.

A Record of an Individual's Grand Challenge VII
Atsushi Kishimoto, age 32, is a cheerful and well-respected medical doctor. However, he was obsessed with being accepted by others and this was shown in his relationship with both his patients and the hospital staff. For example, he would be extremely nice to those patients

who praised him, but would poorly treat those who had complaints against him. With his staff, he always tried to be popular with everyone, going out drinking with the nursing staff or on ski trips with the staff to get on their good side. These relationships were, however, rather shallow, but he felt fulfilled and satisfied by them.

His seeking of instant gratification through these relationships just to fit in or out of conformity is typical of those with the **Pleasure-Lethargy** orientation. Dr. Kishimoto grew up in a well-respected and well-to-do family. However, when he was still a little boy, his father took most of the family's financial resources to start up new companies that seemed to go bankrupt one after the other. These business failures apparently almost drove the father to consider suicide or to flee to a different country.

His father was ostracized by other members of the family and became estranged from them. The young Dr. Kishimoto was protected from this whole situation by his mother, who raised him to believe that it was important to take responsibility, that failures were unacceptable, and that it was important to be loved by everyone. These "silent messages" filtered into Dr. Kishimoto as he was brought up to take over as the bright star of the family.

He chose the medical profession as a career path in part because of the suffering he saw his mother and father go through in his young days. However, after he actually became a doctor, this strong, pure feeling to help heal the mind and body of others gradually disappeared as he became comfortable in his new life. Because a doctor is often treated with great respect and because Dr. Kishimoto constantly sought the approval of his patients and his nurses, he became mired in the delusional reality of **Pleasure-Lethargy**.

But this delusional reality came into full focus when one day a patient with late-stage liver cancer unexpectedly passed away much earlier than predicted. This patient was divorced and Dr. Kishimoto thought that the patient would have wanted to spend his last days back in his old hometown with his family. That he had been unable to prolong the man's life long enough to allow that to happen, made Dr. Kishimoto fully feel the limits of his happy and comfortable life. He vowed to stop acting the "good doctor" and start focusing more on each patient's feelings. Though he had always tried to avoid difficult circumstances at all costs to maintain his comfortable existence, he opted to take a radically different path. He began to take full responsibility for the welfare of his patients, having faith in whatever the outcome. He also began to take a keen interest in the inner pain of each patient, even those who he wasn't officially assigned to, and felt their pain as well.

For example, when he had to treat a woman in her eighties suffering from anemia and lumbago, although he had been routinely visiting her and providing the appropriate medicine, she began complaining he never visited her or gave her medicine. Although his initial reaction was to be defensive, he realized that what the woman was trying to convey to him was that she wanted him to pay closer attention to her inner pain as well. With this incident, he made daily visits to her and attended to her inner pain as well. Amazingly, without any further medical treatment, the woman's condition improved with her hemoglobin level rising to normal. The easing of the patient's inner pain through Dr. Kishimoto's efforts was also shown when she was released from the hospital. Her family, with whom she had had a strained relationship, warmly invited her to live together with them.

Dr. Kishimoto was quite surprised that the body and mind were so intimately connected. Even after this incident, he had numerous encounters in which attending to both the inner and outer pain helped his patients recover. As time went on, he realized that he had been able to return to his original aspiration to be a doctor that could treat both inner and outer ailments. This holistic way to treat suffering, which came from his **true self**, was necessary for Dr. Kishimoto to fulfill his responsibility and role as a member of the human community attempting to heal both his own inner issues as well as the pain in this world of disintegration.

CHAPTER 4

The Inception of the Grand Challenge
(To Look within Ourselves)

	Structure		Keywords
Chapter 1 The Path of Resonating with the Universe	The State of Enlightenment That Pervades All Things (The Underlying Theme)		Six Forces
Chapter 2 A New Paradigm to Understand the Inner and Outer Worlds	The State of Enlightenment (Ultimate Purpose)	The 21st Century The Other Side of the Faultline	Chaos Mind-and-Form Unit
Chapter 3 The Soul Compass	Causes of Suffering (Present Situation-Causes)	The 20th Century This Side of the Faultline	Four Blades
Chapter 4 The Inception of the Grand Challenge (To Look within Ourselves)	The Path (Method-Means)	From the 20th to the 21st Century (Transcending the Faultline)	To Look within Ourselves
Chapter 5 The Inception of the Grand Challenge (To Connect Our Inner Selves and the Outer World)			To Connect Our Inner Selves and the Outer World

From a Small Change to the Grand Challenge

The Search for Truth, the Experiment with Truth, and the Grasping of Truth

In every major transition in human history, there have been those who have imagined and systematized new worldviews and theories of human nature. Although it has never been easy for such people to work out an appropriate view of humanity and the world, they succeeded in creating high ideals that were then spread to all corners of the world so that a major transition could happen for all of humanity.

At a time when violence reigned, Mahatma Gandhi (1869-1948) promoted a vision of Satyagraha, or a Truth-based nonviolence, that led to India's independence. At a time when nurses were looked down upon, Florence Nightingale (1820-1910) regained a sense of pride for the nursing profession and built the foundations for the modern nursing system. At a time when nations were at constant war, Henri Dunant (1828-1910) formed the Red Cross which treated war victims without favor. At a time when smallpox was rampant, Ogata Koan (1810-63), in a novel approach, experimented with cow pus to develop a vaccine to save lives in Japan.

All of these individuals confronted major issues of their times and, through experimentation and creativity, imagined new ways of thinking and living and concrete measures and systems which supported those new ideas and life styles. All of them must have refined these ideas and systems over time, with numerous failures and disappointments, and they set up hypotheses and experimented until they ultimately arrived at a solution which their time called out for. Such is the process wherein the Truth is searched for, experimented with, and finally grasped.

Such a search, for example, can be found in the thought of Immanuel Kant (1724-1804), who searched for how to understand the Absolute or God. While philosophers throughout the ages suggested that the existence of the Absolute or God could be either rationally or experientially proven, Kant suggested that religion lay beyond either of those two methods. Instead he advocated a dimension beyond rational thought or pure reason, a realm of faith. His philosophy exemplifies a life dedicated to the search for Truth.

Gandhi exemplifies someone who dedicated his life to experimenting with Truth, as the subtitle of his famous autobiography suggests. Attempting to find an appropriate response to the British colonization of India, he developed an experiment with the concept of Satyagraha (nonviolent attainment of Truth) in which one developed an inner nonviolence which would flow outward to overcome the violence of the outside world.

Honen (1133-1212), the founder of the so-called Pure Land school of Buddhism in Japan, exemplifies a life dedicated to grasping the Truth. He preached a simple form of Buddhism that focused on the recitation of the Buddha's name. His teachings spread among the common people. This was an amazing development because up until Honen's time, Buddhism was a religion patronized primarily by the elite in society. For the first time, a Buddhist monk went out of his way to blaze an approach to Buddhist practice—the chanting of the Buddha's name—that was truly open to all so that people of all ages, classes, and genders could achieve rebirth in the Buddha's Pure Land. This made available the ability to grasp the Truth for everyone.

The **Grand Challenge** that we now face at the precipice of the 21st century is also an opportunity for us to search for, experiment with, and grasp the Truth. Such a process of coming in contact with the **Grand Challenge** might sound idealist and something far off in the future, but it is not an abstraction but something we must concretely come in touch with. If the **Grand Challenge** is to truly become real for your life, the path we will discover hereafter must be attended to with your whole life experience. Although it is an ideal, it is simultaneously very real. Although it is a calling from the future (the 21st century), it is simultaneously something that must be understood and practiced in the here and now.

Human Attitudes That Appear with the Change in Values

As we look back on the values that sustained the 20th century, we can broadly divide them into "materials," "energy," and "information." Items that we assign value to, categorized this way, could be represented by the following items: bread, kerosene, and CDs (compact disks). Because we give them value, we pay hard-earned money for them. We give bread value because it provides sustenance for our food needs. We give kerosene value because it generates energy and light. We give CDs value because on a small piece of aluminum, they can hold vast amounts of information. In each of these, we can see how a 20th-century paradigm of values is embedded.

Bread or any other agricultural "materials" are fundamentally blessings given to us by the earth. However, going against the flow and pace of nature, we humans have developed all kinds of techniques to speed up the process of farming such "materials" for our benefit. Through artificial breeding techniques and genetic engineering, we have tried to squeeze as many things out of nature as possible, ignoring the effects on the earth. The attitude or value that underlies such developments is the concept that one need not look within (at the human) to solve problems, but only depend on external solutions.

As for energy, a similar value of looking outside ourselves has dominated human activity. Ignoring the energies that dwell within each of us, we have spent much money and human resources in researching and developing new techniques for increasing external energy sources to sustain our life styles. To develop the energies within the human has been at best a side issue.

With information, with the explosion of the Internet, it is now possible to have a vast amount of information on all kinds of conceivable topics in an instant from around the world. But in reality, the actual amount of information on even such a vast network of information that is really essential for our inner selves is quite minimal. Although "information" is something that should rather naturally connect with our inner mind, instead of doing so, most of us seem to live in a world of information that swirls around us in a haphazard way.

The Grand Challenge of Our Age : To Look within Ourselves and to Connect Our Inner Selves and the Outer World

According to the futurist Alvin Toffler, the three values we discussed above represent stages or waves in human development and value formation (see Chart 14). The First Wave was characterized by agriculture with value given to material products. But with the invention of the steam locomotive in 1712, the 1879 invention of the electric bulb, and the beginnings of the mass production of cars in 1908, the value of energy started to emerge. This era, the Second Wave, has been called

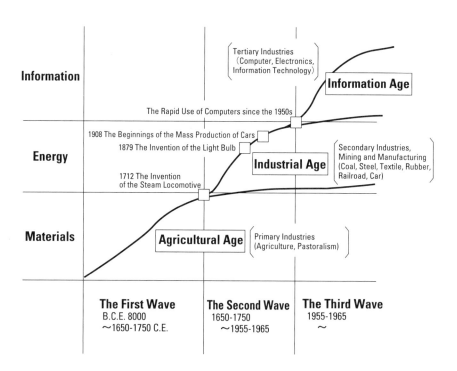

Chart 14 : The Three Waves and the Three Shifts

the industrial age. Finally, with the rapid use of computers since the 1950s, the Third Wave information age characterized by value given to information appeared.

Although these three waves in human history certainly represent major shifts in modes of production and value, they all fundamentally share the same paradigm when viewed from our perspective. While finding new approaches to deal with shifting material realities, all three shifts or dropping away of the old ideas retained the fundamental value of **ignoring the inner world** in favor of **changing only the outer world**. They thus represent "small changes" in contrast to the change we envision for the 21st century which is the **Grand Challenge**.

While we cannot but recognize the progress made through these waves in human history, nevertheless, we must also be mindful of their pitfalls. The economic development or the technological advances also had their shadow with the maintenance of a greed-filled, spiritless system leading to the depletion of the earth's natural resources and putting the whole earth's balance into question. What we are proposing here is to make a radical and fundamental shift away from the whole structure which underlies the so-called "small changes" based on self-centered principles.

Meetings such as the recently-held Kyoto convention on climate change, at which 160 countries and regions discussed questions of how to create practical solutions to the depletion of the ozone layer, reflect growing concern about humanity's course. How have we allowed ourselves to come so close to destroying the very basis of life? Our inability to go beyond the 20th-century mindset of **ignoring the inner world** and **changing only the outer world** is surely the basic root of this problem. Because of our worldview we have continually created negative cycles of destruction that have been destroying this earth.

We must not take our old mindset into the new millennium. The old "small changes" will not allow us to transcend the faultline between the 20th and 21st centuries. For the new millennium, we need a new paradigm—**to look within ourselves** and **to connect our inner selves and the outer world** (see Chart 15). The **Grand Challenge** presented by the world to us today is to create a different world based on the new 21st-century paradigm. This paradigm is not a new technique to deal with reality, but something far more fundamental that needs to be

The 20th-Century Paradigm	The 21st-Century Paradigm
To Ignore the Inner World To Change Only the Outer World	To Look within Ourselves To Connect Our Inner Selves and the Outer World

Chart 15 : The Two Principles Underlying the 20th and 21st Centuries

shifted at the base of our way of thinking and acting.

Everyone Faces Chaos

Although the phrases **to look within ourselves** and **to connect our inner selves and the outer world** seem easy enough, they are extremely difficult for us because we don't really know what it means to introspectively investigate ourselves and we have not received any prior training in connecting our inner selves and the outer world. Because we have lived for so long with the paradigm of **ignoring the inner world** while **changing only the outer world**, we have come to cut our inner selves off from the outer world. The new paradigm asks us to reconnect the two worlds, which were originally inextricably linked.

As we link these two worlds, as we have already discussed, we must face **chaos** straight on and learn that how we face it determines the course of future events. For a businessman, **chaos** may appear in everyday business dealings. For an educator, a troubled youth walking down the hall may represent **chaos** in living form and how to deal with this youth represents an opportunity to deal with **chaos** itself. Whatever shape **chaos** may take for us, we must face straight up to it to be able to begin our **Grand Challenge** journey. The **Grand Challenge** is also about overcoming the **four personality types** and **four blades** we discussed in Chapter 3. We need to overcome the **four personality types** and **four blades** because they are based on a fundamentally misguided view that the inner self and the outer world are two separate things. To do so requires the letting go of our old traditions and habits which inhibit us from true wisdom and love. Using the **soul compass**, we must reconnect the various ways in which our inner selves and the outer world have been cut off by the **four false selves** and **four blades**.

To Overcome the Conflict between the 20th and 21st Centuries

For anyone who embarks on the **Grand Challenge**, there always appears a great barrier. It is never easy to shift away from our old, routinized ways of thinking to a new paradigm. To live in a new way will sometimes feel uncomfortable and it is to be expected that one will also feel a pullback toward the old paradigms represented by the four blades. In other words, the 20th-century and 21st-century paradigms are in conflict with each other during our journey.

The old paradigms are at once both our personal patterns of behavior as well as representing the 20th-century's old way of thinking. The 21st century, therefore, is not a far-off reality, but it flows out from our **true self** freed from the **four blades** and old paradigms. We will begin our lives in the 21st century right here, right now as we shed the old and enliven the new. However small our first steps, as we embark on this journey, the 21st century will come alive in each and every one of us.

The Practice of the Grand Challenge I : To Look within Ourselves

Self-Diagnosis Chart

The two key paradigms, **to look within ourselves** and **to connect our inner selves and the outer world**, are concepts that need very concrete forms to understand and put them into practice. Let us first take up the practice of looking within ourselves. The initial step in such a self-diagnosis is to figure out which of the **four personality types**, discussed in Chapter 3, is dominant within ourselves.

Use the following self-diagnosis list to see which ones fit you:

1] I get angry or defiant when given criticism that sounds unfair.
2] I'm proud of my way of life and accomplishments.
3] I become depressed when something bad happens.
4] I attach importance to being conflict- and problem-free.
5] I get terribly disappointed when I look back on my life.
6] I want to do things as I desire.
7] I hold unforgiving feelings toward my parents.
8] I think that my life is stable when I look back on it.
9] I think I'm good at doing things.
10] I'm told by others that I'm absent-minded.
11] I quickly feel like a victim or that things are unfair.
12] I'm anxious about what people will say about me.
13] I believe I'm calm and collected.
14] Fearful of failure, I run away quickly from bad situations.
15] I feel a strong boost whenever I move up in society.
16] I hold a strong impression that everyone has good and evil sides.
17] I'm frequently told by others that they are afraid of me.

18] I feel that things would go better if people gave me more responsibility.

19] I feel resigned to the result if I gave it my best.

20] I cannot voice my opinion because I don't want to be hated by others.

21] I cannot stand losing to others.

22] Looking back on my life, there is at least one person I cannot ever forgive.

23] I always have had someone who would protect me.

24] I always have feelings of self-deprecation.

25] I often give up even before starting.

26] I feel it's more important that everyone gets along than risk ill feelings by being innovative.

27] I'm drawn to historical figures like heroes and geniuses.

28] People can easily tell when I'm angry.

29] I feel out of sorts if I'm not the center of attention.

30] I feel it's strong-willed to never give in.

31] I feel I'm not obsessed about anything.

32] I feel it's better not to do anything than cause trouble to others.

Now, let's compile the results by using Chart 16. Put a check mark in the box assigned to each of the 32 items that you feel describes you. Then mark down the total checkmarks for each column in A, B, C, and D. Then put these totals into Chart 17. The higher the number of marks, the more likely that you are this personality type. Did any of the personality types come up as particularly representative for you?

Immediate Feeling, Perception, Thoughts, and Action

The next step in our self-diagnosis **to look within ourselves** is to understand the processes which make up our **mind-and-form unit**. In other words, we must understand our tendencies as we experience immediate feelings, our perceptions of them, our ways of thinking about them, and our subsequent actions. This is difficult, in part, because these four movements occur almost one after the other in the space of an instant. These four stages in our mind correspond to senses, emotions, thinking, and volition, which are not only difficult to grasp, but even more difficult to stop or change.

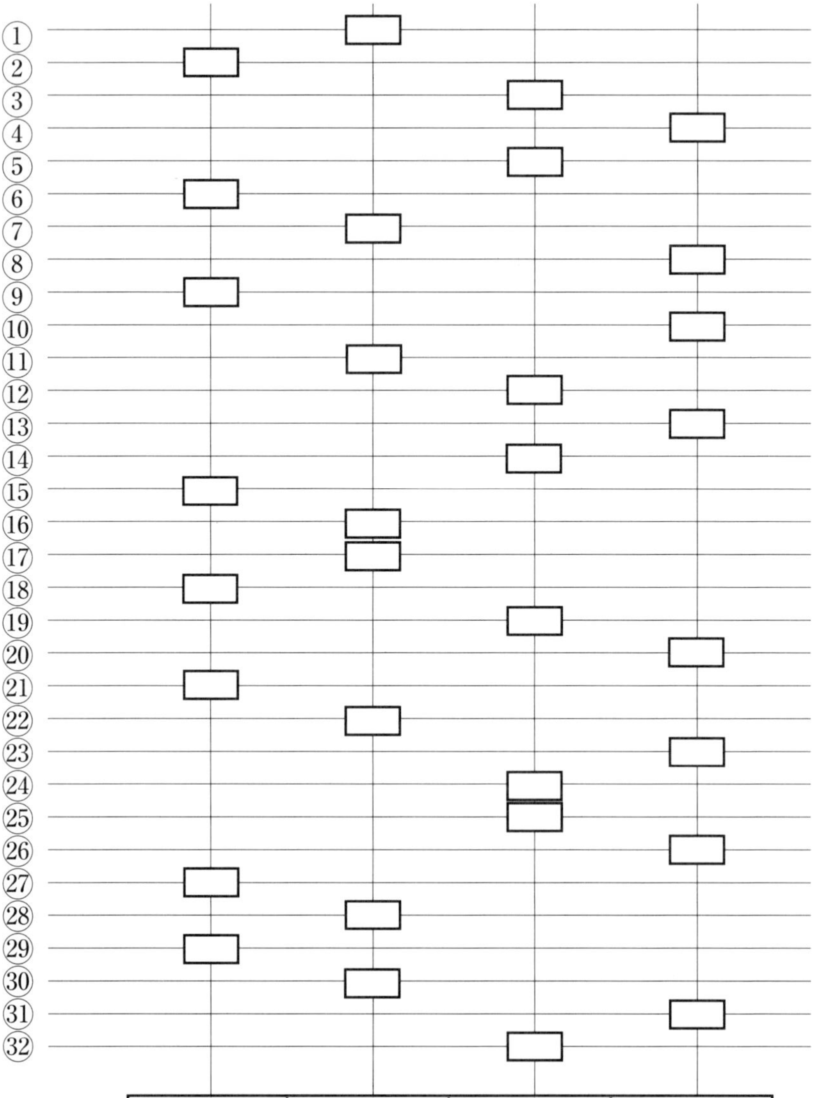

A	B	C	D

Chart 16 : Self-Diagnosis List Composite Result Sheet

A	**Over-Confident Type**	
B	**Resentful Victim Type**	
C	**Self-Depreciating Type**	
D	**Self-Satisfied Type**	

7-8 Points : Very High Likelihood of Being This Type
5-6 Points : High Likelihood of Being This Type
3-4 Points : A Lower Likelihood of Being This Type
0-2 Points : Unlikely to Be This Type

Chart 17 : Self-Diagnosis List Composite Result Sheet

To look deeply within ourselves, therefore, requires a method. Buddhists have, from ancient times, practiced a method of stopping one's thought-filled mind for reflection and then engaging in insight meditation or deeply looking within themselves. Literally meaning to "stop and see," the technique of "Shikan" allows us to reflect on the nature of our **immediate feeling**, **perception**, **thoughts**, **and action** and to obtain deep insight into their nature. This process is a spiritual discipline and education which allows us to see the Truth.

The Reflections and Insight Sheet

Just as correct diagnosis is the basis for finding an appropriate cure in medicine, correctly understanding our **immediate feeling**, **perception**, **thoughts**, **and action** is crucial to examining and slowly changing our patterned behavior. For this, we can use the **Reflections and Insight Sheet,** or Shikan Sheet (Chart 18).

To use the sheet correctly, first start by writing in a particular incident that has happened to you in the recent past. Then, write down the raw or immediate feeling you experienced in that incident such as "Oh" or "Hmm."

Next, write down the shape that this experience took, in other words, your initial perception of the incident with words like "Why?" or "Oh my gosh!" The words that would most often appear here would be terms associated with either pleasure or pain. In the third step, you should record your thoughts that ran through your mind. And finally, record any actions that you took because of the incident.

In the bottom half of the sheet, take note of any "murmurs" or remarks that you often repeat to yourself when confronted with similar incidents. Finally, you can become aware of when you notice and put a brake on these cyclical events. Recording these thought processes on the Sheet in a cumulative manner allows you to understand your inner personality more clearly.

But of course, simply understanding ourselves is not the final goal. The purpose of this technique is to change ourselves by getting to know ourselves better. We need to constantly question our **true self** regarding what we really ought to have done in the context of the incident. This process of accessing our true self in times like this can be made easier if we use another book of mine, *The Path of Prayer*,

SHIKAN SHEET
Reflections and Insight Sheet

Incident

Immediate Feeling

↓

Perception

↓

Thoughts

↓

Action

Murmurs Coming Out from the Incident

Where Will You Stop and Reflect Next Time?

© KEIKO TAKAHASHI

Chart 18 : SHIKAN SHEET (Reflections and Insight Sheet)

together with this **Reflections and Insight Sheet**.

The Immediate Feelings, Perceptions, Thoughts, and Actions of the Four False Selves

There are a number of pattern ways in which **immediate feeling, perception, thoughts, and action** appear in each of the **four false selves**. In Buddhism, it is said that there are 108 unhealthy desires. These represent the range of human delusion and greed that distract us from the Path. Although there are so many desires outlined in Buddhism, they can generally be categorized into four major types as shown in Chart 19 (which can be divided along the two axes of **Pleasure-Pain** and **Recklessness-Lethargy**). Using the **soul compass**, these patterns can be recognized as a way to understand our inner world as composed of archetypal ways in which we experience **immediate feeling, perception, thoughts, and action**.

Once we are drawn into any of these four patterns, typically our thought processes automatically go through the sequence outlined in the chart. Even though reality may present us with many options and choices, these patterns make us believe and act as if there were only one way to understand and act on a situation. Thus, to become free from these patterns, we must first of all become aware of what the patterns are and how they appear in each one of us. Understanding and changing these patterns allow a new **mind-and-form unit** to emerge that will open us up to a new world of possibilities. Below we will take up several cases of people who have used the **Reflections and Insight Sheet** and *The Path of Prayer* to transform their lives.

Records of the Grand Challenge

A Record of an Individual's Grand Challenge VIII

Akio Yanagawa, age 53, runs a law office in Tokyo. He was a well-respected lawyer in his neighborhood who had worked hard at his job. Though he seemed quite successful, there was something empty about his life. He began questioning the purpose of his life now that he had been able to establish his earlier goals of gaining status and prestige in his community. He wondered if there weren't something more to life. But at this juncture in his life, there was no way for him to really figure

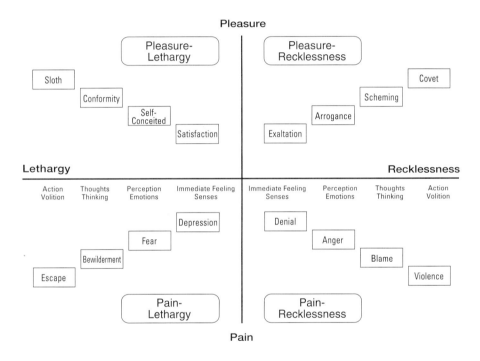

**Chart 19 : The Four Patterns of Immediate
Feeling, Perception, Thoughts, and Action**

out this question. It was only after he started working with the **Reflections and Insight Sheet** on a daily basis that he began the journey of self-discovery.

Mr. Yanagawa's father was a self-made man who, through hard work and dedication, pulled himself up by his bootstraps. Mr. Yanagawa was born as a long-awaited son to this outgoing father. People around him treated the young Mr. Yanagawa as a prince. He just sat there and food and silverware seemed to magically appear. Other people's expectations of the young boy were high. And hoping to meet their expectations, he studied hard which resulted in his law career. All this bred the **Over-Confident** personality type which led to a somewhat snobbish attitude toward others.

This attitude, however, only created distance between himself and others. Unable to live intimately and authentically, he developed an outer mask that he would wear when together with others. However, his recognition of these patterns began when he started to write **Reflections and Insight Sheets** on a regular basis. A typical example of Mr. Yanagawa's early Sheet, representative of his initial pattern, can be found in Figure 15. On it, he first described the "incident" or the context of what happened. In this case, he had ordered one of his employees earlier in the day to do an errand at a town office in the late afternoon. However, while his employee was out on a different errand in the morning, it came to Mr. Yanagawa's attention that a more pressing errand needed to be done in the afternoon. So when the employee returned to the law office, Mr. Yanagawa, without explaining the change, told him to cancel the first set of instructions and to get over to the more urgent situation. The employee quickly replied, "OK."

Mr. Yanagawa's most "immediate feeling" was "Um" and his "perception" of the situation was "That's Good." When he began to think about it, his "thoughts" were, "He listened to me properly. That's the way it should be. Even though his assignments may change, his job is to simply accept my orders. This is what work is all about." As for the "action" that he took regarding the situation, Mr. Yanagawa simply kept on with his work and nodded to himself that everything was fine.

By writing in Sheets like this everyday, Mr. Yanagawa was able to see his own snobbish attitude in his thought patterns. He also saw that he had a shallow and distant relationship with that particular employee.

SHIKAN SHEET
Reflections and Insight Sheet

Incident

Without explaining the situation, told an employee to cancel
my first set of instructions to get over to a more urgent situation.
He told me "OK."

Immediate Feeling

Um.

↓

Perception

That's Good.

↓

Thoughts

He listened to me properly. That's the way it should be.
Even though his assignments may change, his job is to simply
accept my orders. This is what work is all about.

↓

Action

Simply kept on with my work and nodded to myself that everything
was fine.

Murmurs Coming Out from the Incident

There's no mistake as long as people do as I say.
There's no need to unnecessarily talk to me.
It's no use to explain things in detail.

Where Will You Stop and Reflect Next Time?

Focus on the perception "That's Good."

Figure 15 : Mr. Yanagawa's Reflections and Insight Sheet

As he saw in his "murmur," "There's no mistake as long as people do as I say," his condescending attitude put fear into those around him. This led to a drop in their motivation and to a distancing between him and others. This distance and disconnection between each other's true feelings meant that relationships could only be very shallow. The possibility of resentment growing was also high, he reflected, as he recalled an incident in which someone who had been treated in this high-handed way for some time suddenly blew up at him.

This process of self-discovery developed over time for Mr. Yanagawa as he continued this practice of writing in his **Reflections and Insight Sheets** on a regular basis. He was further able to accept his imperfections with the help of *The Path of Prayer*, which can be used as a practical companion volume. He especially began using page 197 of the book, the section on "When You Are in a State of Exaltation." There is a line there, "Is the joy that now fills your heart a joy which arises from the core of your soul? Or is it a momentary excitation?" Repeating this phrase numerous times to himself, he slowly began to find his **true self**. He realized that what he really wanted was to be an unpretentious, genuine person, rather than the snob that he had become.

These days, Mr. Yanagawa's relationships are more authentic and based on his faith in his own and the other people's deepest selves, their divine nature. Having contact with other people has become fun for him with his newfound confidence from the center of his soul, rather than a superimposed confidence of times past. This confidence led him to also reestablish relationships with his sibling, with whom he had had only a strained connection. His self-discovery propelled a turn toward the light as he managed to sincerely approach his sibling again.

At work, things have also changed. While in the past, his only concern was with properly filling out the paperwork for his clients, these days, he has opened up to his clients' inner worries as well as their legal problems. His work has become, then, not just a duty, but a passionate forum for him to help out those in need. Because being a lawyer is a business often based on trust, his change has brought on more and more clients as he has gained a reputation as a lawyer who cares.

A Record of an Individual's Grand Challenge IX

The **Grand Challenge** can also begin from a small problem of every-day life. Ms. Satoko Sawaguchi, age 50, is a homemaker, who was going through a difficult period in her marriage to her husband, Toshio. Although they had married out of love, their hearts drifted away from each other over time. Ms. Sawaguchi blamed her husband, constantly thinking, "If he were only more of a man!" She developed a victim mentality thinking that any and all of her troubles were her husband's fault. As for the husband, he seemed to collapse into a more and more unresponsive position as time went on.

The more they tried to talk about it, the more distant they seemed to grow. Their two children also started fighting with each other, making for a terrible atmosphere at home. During this period, Ms. Sawaguchi even contemplated divorce.

Ms. Sawaguchi grew up in a relatively well-off family which had very strong family values. Her father was well-educated and a wealthy landowner and her mother, the daughter of a high school principal. But from a fairly young age, Ms. Sawaguchi felt that she didn't fit in and was the black sheep of the family. It started at age four when her younger sister was born. Her father had entered the room to see the newborn child and when Ms. Sawaguchi tried to follow him, a door was slammed in her face. Further, she didn't look at all like her mother, who was sophisticated and elegant, though her younger sisters strikingly resembled their mother.

Trying to receive the attention of her parents, she started to act wild and used bad words. However, such rebelliousness led to further strain and distance between them. She even began thinking that she must have been orphaned and adopted into the family. Going on to design school, she met her future husband Toshio, who seemed to accept and understand her. Feeling that she could go through life with him, she married him thinking that she finally found a place for herself. But as mentioned above, their relationship started to crumble because of miscommunication and misunderstanding. Though she hoped for him to be a sturdier man, he only seemed to get weaker. Before she knew it, 20 years of this type of life had passed and she basically came to accept this awkward situation.

Their marriage, however, began to take a turn toward the better after they started to write **Reflections and Insight Sheets** on a regular basis. A typical example of their early Sheet can be found in Figure 16.

With this case and many other such Sheets, Ms. Sawaguchi recognized a consistent pattern wherein she would get upset and mutter something before concluding that her husband was in the wrong. She thought that because she was always in the right and her husband in the wrong, these situations would resolve themselves if her husband would attempt to make changes. This thought process is typical of those with the **Resentful Victim** personality type (**Pain-Recklessness**).

And what about her husband? His Sheets consistently included phrases such as "Stop nagging me. Don't always make it my fault, what about you? But if I say anything back now, you'll only nag me more, so I'd better keep my mouth closed. If you didn't press me so much, things would be fine." In terms of what he did about these situations, he would simply tried to ride out the tirade or change the subject. What seemed like nagging to her husband was, for Ms. Sawaguchi, a natural response to a husband who seemed to be ignoring her and not caring about what she was saying. This cycle of pressing and escape, pressing and escape, became like a terrible whirlpool pulling the relationship down the drain.

What became clear when the couple's Sheets were seen together was that Ms. Sawaguchi's pressing did not solve any of the situations, but only laid the seeds for destruction. Furthermore, both of them had the attitude that if only the other person would change, everything would be better. Based on this thought, one can notice the huge amounts of energy expended in trying to change the other person's behavior. Realizing that her 20 years of always blaming her husband was misguided, Ms. Sawaguchi took the first step of trying to change her way of thinking and acting. It started with a fairly straightforward, but concrete step of stopping herself in a moment when she would normally have gotten angry at her husband and instead evoking a feeling of love and understanding and using kind words.

Using the companion volume, *The Path of Prayer*, the section "When You Become Angry" on page 33, helped her: "Is there any fear or humiliation deep inside your heart? . . . May I change the heat and force of anger / To the strength to forbear / To the strength to wait / To the strength to love." She faced her victim mentality with these

SHIKAN SHEET
Reflections and Insight Sheet

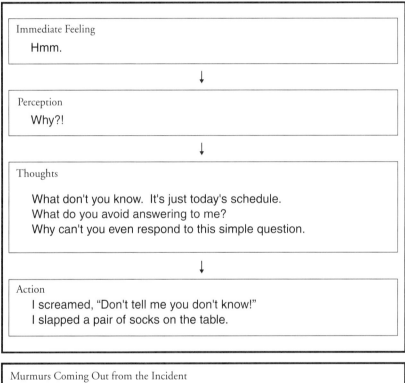

Incident

Morning. Asked my husband what his schedule was for today.
He told me he didn't know.

Immediate Feeling

Hmm.

↓

Perception

Why?!

↓

Thoughts

What don't you know. It's just today's schedule.
What do you avoid answering to me?
Why can't you even respond to this simple question.

↓

Action

I screamed, "Don't tell me you don't know!"
I slapped a pair of socks on the table.

Murmurs Coming Out from the Incident

How vexing!
He's making fun of me!

Where Will You Stop and Reflect Next Time?

Focus on the perception "Why."

© KEIKO TAKAHASH

Figure 16 : Ms. Sawaguchi's Reflections and Insight Sheet

words as a prayer.

Eventually, their marriage began to heal and become stronger. At times when she ordinarily would have gotten upset, Ms. Sawaguchi instead patiently strove to feel love and use kind words. Her husband responded to her efforts by opening up to her more than ever before. What had at first been a tremendous effort to seem kind and use loving words soon became natural and second nature to her.

The improved relationship between husband and wife expanded outwards to include their children. The siblings who were formerly constantly fighting with each other stopped. Ms. Sawaguchi was finally able to discover her own place in the world as this family continues their practice of implementing the **Grand Challenge** day by day.

A Record of an Individual's Grand Challenge X

Junichi Mukai, age 60, is a professor of engineering at a university. Although university professors should be comfortable dealing with people, one of Professor Mukai's greatest fears was getting up and giving a lecture in front of a group. He would stare at his notes and the blackboard to deliver his talk, never looking out at his students. At faculty meetings, he was so scared of how he would sound to others, he rarely said anything. This was a form of people-phobia.

Professor Mukai lost his mother at the young age of nine months. Even during her pregnancy, his mother, being afflicted with tuberculosis, had nearly been unable to go through with the birth. Born underweight, he was afflicted with numerous ailments as a baby and did not utter his first words until age four. His childhood was a lonely and isolated one, even though he had the one thing he was good at: studying to get good grades. Always mistrusting others, his fear of what others would think of him led him to put all his efforts in the one path he thought open to him, studying.

However, one incident in particular sticks out in his student days that exemplified his personality. At a student party one night, when it came to be his turn to introduce himself, his mind went completely blank. Left there standing like a fool, his inability to speak out came to humiliate and haunt him. On every subsequent occasion when he had to speak in front of others, he had a flashback to that college party and the same fears would bubble up within him. Thus, for him to have become a university professor was a rather strange twist of fate. Every lecture or faculty meeting ended up becoming like a nightmare for him.

It was then that he immersed himself in writing **Reflections and Insight Sheets**. In the space of a couple of years, he had filled out approximately 1,400 such Sheets. Every morning, he would write down incidents from the previous day and also used *The Path of Prayer* to give these incidents some context.

Slowly this practice began to show its fruits. A trip to Nairobi in Kenya, where he was assigned to a technological assistance team, exemplified this transition in his life. When he was in Japan, he could depend on or escape to his family or friends in troubled times. But in Nairobi, all alone, the only thing he could rely on was the **Reflections and Insight Sheet** and *The Path of Prayer*.

It was toward the end of his stay there, after he had completed his part for the technological program, that he was suddenly overwhelmed with doubts about his project. Even though he was about to depart back to Japan the following week, once this worrying began, there was no stopping it. He stayed up all night and his worries can be seen in the following **Reflections and Insight Sheet** (see Figure 17).

Because of his anxiety, he turned to the "When You Are Anxious and Afraid" section of *The Path of Prayer* and read it over and over before realizing how pitiful his whole attitude had been. He saw just how small his "world" had been and just how pitiful and sad it was that he had worried so. The thick veil that had covered Professor Mukai, which was the veil of **Pain-Lethargy** itself, was pierced by a clear light in that moment when he read *The Path of Prayer*. This light is the healing light that envelops all things, it it the light of Truth. This light from the **true self** shone upon the dark covering of the **false self** and stopped the incessant movement of the blade of **Pain-Lethargy**.

At this time, he wrote some insightful sentences on the back of his Sheet, "I want to be valued highly by others, so failures are unacceptable. This thought has been a theme throughout my life. I've always been searching to find a way not to fail, but in fact, there is no such path. I need to accept that I'm going to fail sometimes. I need to be able to

SHIKAN SHEET
Reflections and Insight Sheet

Incident

At night, can't stop thinking about the possibility of failure at the project.

Immediate Feeling
Oh dear!

↓

Perception
This is no good anymore!

↓

Thoughts

Everyone's probably making fun of me behind my back, especially the people at Jomo Kenyatta University. What am I supposed to do?

↓

Action

Ceaselessly asked God to please help me.

Murmurs Coming Out from the Incident

This is no good anymore!

Where Will You Stop and Reflect Next Time?

Focus on the perception "This is no good anymore!"

© KEIKO TAKAHASHI

Figure 17 : Mr. Mukai's Reflections and Insight Sheet

live together with this anxiety." That night when he couldn't sleep was one when he realized that if his project was not going to be a success, he should admit it forthrightly instead of holding onto a fear-driven sense of pride.

Professor Mukai, even after this particular incident, continued to faithfully fill out **Reflections and Insight Sheets**. And before long, it dawned upon him that he was having fun being with other people. What he had feared the most became a source of great joy for him. At school, as well, he could honestly say that he enjoyed being around and conversing with his students.

Today, in his department, people say that it is hard to tell whether he is an engineering professor or a counselor because of his love for talking and helping others. He came to realize that precisely because of his suffering and alienation of his youth, he was in a perfect position to talk to students who were experiencing that type of loneliness. His joy and confidence also functioned in his research and in his family life as well. When he feared a project failure similar to the one in Nairobi some years later, he was able to deal with it much better. In terms of his family, the distance that existed between himself and his children, for example, disappeared.

His life had turned around 180 degrees and the once fearful professor had become a person who could accept the hurt of others with sympathy. This is the type of result that can come about with the help of **Reflections and Insight Sheet**.

A Record of an Individual's Grand Challenge XI

Hisao Kinouchi, age 47, is the head of a major industrial materials supplier in the Kansai region of Japan. Mr. Kinouchi was the eighth-generation president of his company which had been a family-run business for over 200 years. Born as the first son, he was looked after by his parents and others to be groomed to take over the company when his time came. Both his parents were well-respected in the community, known for their generosity and well-cultured ways.

Born into such a situation, his personality soon turned toward a **Self-Satisfied** type moved by **Pleasure-Lethargy**. He valued hierarchical relationships and distance between himself and others. Looking back on his early years, Mr. Kinouchi has reflected that he was happy, but that this pleasure was a self-contained one, cut off from the concerns and pains of others. When he became president of the firm, therefore, he found that he cut himself off from those who worked in his family business, including those that were incompetent or didn't work according to the company's overall objectives.

In the company, there was a sales department which had for the past 25 years shown declining productivity. It was thought that there was no hope for reviving this consistently poor-performer. However, as president, he wanted to see how this department which hadn't turned a profit in years was connected to his own inner attitude and mind.

So he decided to write out a **Reflections and Insight Sheet** with his thoughts on a mid-ranking department supervisor (see Figure 18). This particular supervisor, roughly 40 years old, had been with the firm for seventeen years. Mr. Kinouchi noted how this man had poor results on the job and very little trust within the company. Compared to those who had entered the firm at the same time, his productivity was less than a third. He never reached the targeted sales goal and always lost market share for the company.

Although Mr. Kinouchi noticed that he always reacted with the perception that "This is no good!" he ultimately ended up concluding that there was nothing that could be done and so always gave his seal of approval on the daily logbook. This reaction was premised on his knowledge that the company was doing well overall so this problem could be swept under the rug. Trying not to cause any waves, in a slothful state of apathy developed over the years, he continued in a self-satisfied manner.

But Mr. Kinouchi began the process of reflecting on the fact that this inner attitude of his was hurting and not helping the supervisor do better. He began thinking that he wanted some way to connect with this supervisor. This started with a more careful examination of the supervisor's logbook. When the supervisor came back from his sales rounds, Mr. Kinouchi also took the effort to try to talk with the man to see how things were going. These conversations about the sales and how the supervisor was relating to his clients and so forth began a series of transformations in the supervisor toward a more positive direction.

The change in the man could be seen, first off, in the daily log-

SHIKAN SHEET

Reflections and Insight Sheet

Incident

The supervisor's daily logbook noted that his department only sold a few components to three clients.

Immediate Feeling

Huh.

↓

Perception

Hopeless!

↓

Thoughts

It's the same as always. Is this the extent of his sales after making pitches all day driving around? Nothing changes even if everyone asks him about his sales. It's the same year after year. It's impossible. Isn't he ashamed given that everyone else is working so hard! Maybe it's a mistake to expect anything from him. It's not my business anymore. How troublesome!

↓

Action

I gave my seal of approval on his daily logbook report.

Murmurs Coming Out from the Incident

It's impossible. Oh, I guess there's nothing that can be done.

Where Will You Stop and Reflect Next Time?

Need to more perceptively grasp my immediate feelings.

© KEIKO TAKAHASHI

Figure 18 : Mr. Kinouchi's Reflections and Insight Sheet

book. While previously, there had been periods when the supervisor had skipped two or three out of three days of recording, now each day's report was fuller and more detailed than ever before. Mr. Kinouchi also began to experience a transformation as he waited late at night to see how the supervisor was feeling after his daily sales rounds. He also began thinking, "I want to somehow help this guy out," "This company would be a whole lot better if he could turn his department around," "He must have suffered over those long years working in a depressed department like this," or "Let's think about this together."

That summer, which is generally the off-season for component procurement, a major deal was signed with a certain company. The person responsible for this deal was the formerly troubled supervisor. This company's purchase ranked in the top ten during the first half of the year. So for the first time ever, the supervisor was called to give a report to the Board regarding the sales department. This was because his sales efforts helped the company balance out poor summer sales in the other departments. The supervisor's department, which had in the past been a drag on the company, overwhelmed the sales targets of other departments and helped sustain the company as a whole.

Although Mr. Kinouchi had previously thought that ignoring the man was a minor issue, he came to understand that he was actually neglecting his duties by relating to the supervisor in that way. He came to regret his earlier inaction regarding the situation. Using the Sheet and a passage from the "When You Are Bothered by Shame" section of *The Path of Prayer*, "Isn't it necessary to do selflessly what you think is right and what you think is needed?" he used these words as a guide to go within and reveal his **true self**.

CHAPTER 5

The Inception of the Grand Challenge
(To Connect Our Inner Selves and the Outer World)

	Structure		Keywords
Chapter 1 The Path of Resonating with the Universe	The State of Enlightenment That Pervades All Things （The Underlying Theme）		Six Forces
Chapter 2 A New Paradigm to Understand the Inner and Outer Worlds	The State of Enlightenment （Ultimate Purpose）	The 21st Century The Other Side of the Faultline	Chaos Mind-and-Form Unit
Chapter 3 The Soul Compass	Causes of Suffering （Present Situation-Causes）	The 20th Century This Side of the Faultline	Four Blades
Chapter 4 The Inception of the Grand Challenge （To Look within Ourselves）	The Path （Method-Means）	From the 20th to the 21st Century （Transcending the Faultline）	To Look within Ourselves
Chapter 5 The Inception of the Grand Challenge （To Connect Our Inner Selves and the Outer World）			To Connect Our Inner Selves and the Outer World

The Practice of the Grand Challenge II : To Connect Our Inner Selves and the Outer World

The Bright Light Emerges in Its Splendor

The second part of the **Grand Challenge** is **to connect our inner selves and the outer world** together. In the previous chapter we discussed the ways to shed the veils that cover our true selves. In this chapter, we will be exploring how to connect our true selves to the world, or to be more precise, how to connect and resonate with the **six forces** which fill the entire universe. In other words, the bright light that we discover as the true part of our inner world needs to be directed outward to shine upon the outer world. The bright light emerges in its splendor in this connection between our inner selves and the outer world.

In-En-Kahoh

Before we can connect our inner selves and the outer world, we must first study the principle of **In-En-Kahoh** (**inner cause-environmental conditions-result**). To explain this idea, let us take the example of a flower (see Figure 19). For a flower to grow, it first requires an **In** (**inner cause**) which is the bulb or seed. But the bulb or seed by itself cannot become a flower. The bulb requires **En** (**environmental conditions**), such as soil, water, and oxygen (in other words an environment), to propel its growth into a flower. The **Kahoh** (**result**) is a flower which is the result of the interconnection between **In** and **En**, **inner cause** and **environmental conditions**. Another simple example would be the sound of a drum. This requires as an **In** the drum itself and the **En** of the drumstick, which when put together produce the **Kahoh** or **result** of the sound of a drum.

Reality often appears to us as a mess or an intertwining of strands of strings which are hard to identify. But within the mess that appears before us often lies an order and structure which can be discerned through the notion of **In-En-Kahoh**. Just as we can discern through investigation that a flower owes its existence to a causative factor (flower bulb) and to a variety of conditions (water, soil, and oxygen), the various incidents and events in our lives can be similarly analyzed. When we look at a flower, only when we look deeply using the analyti-

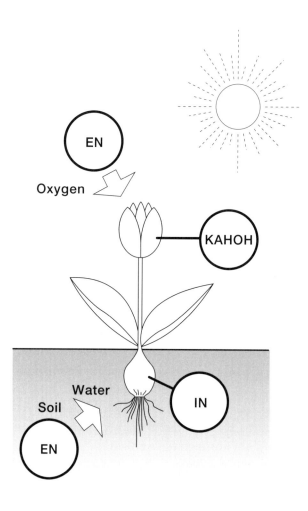

Figure 19 : In-En-Kahoh

cal tool of **In-En-Kahoh**, can we see its true nature.

Our understanding of the ways of **In-En-Kahoh** is also related to our gradual grasping of the reality of our **mind-and-form units** discussed previously. The following are three stages in which the two practices are connected.

Stage 1 : Only the Result (Kahoh) Appears

Before we first truly understand how everything appears from our **mind-and-form units**, reality simply appears as "reality." Without understanding the causes of why this reality appears before us or the interconnections of this reality to other realities, the first stage is a simplistic view of the world in which only the "result" (**Kahoh**) is perceived.

For a businessman, seeing only the **Kahoh** means that reality equals his company and the employees. For a doctor, reality would be the hospital and the patients, while for an educator, the school and the students. At this stage there is no perception that reality is also created by internal factors found in the inner world.

Stage 2 : Understanding of Cause-and-Effect Appears

In the next stage, we develop a sense of "reality" as constituted of **cause** (our inner selves) and **effect** (the outer world). Especially in simple cases, such as straightforward one-to-one relationships or events that emerged from a short duration, we begin to be able to see how "reality" (**effect**) is driven by our mind (**cause**).

Stage 3 : Understanding of In-En-Kahoh (Inner Cause-Environmental Conditions-Result) Appears

However, for complex realities, such as those formed over long periods of time or through interconnections with other realities, the simplistic cause-and-effect formula is not sufficient to understand reality properly. This is when it is necessary to see how reality (**Kahoh–result**) is constructed by our mind (**In–inner cause**) in the environment of various factors (**En–environmental conditions**).

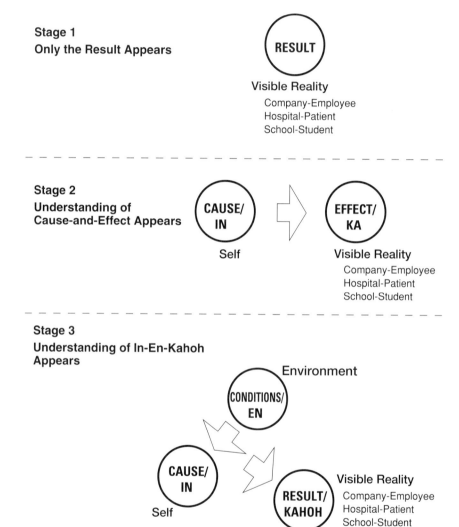

Stage 1
Only the Result Appears

RESULT

Visible Reality
Company-Employee
Hospital-Patient
School-Student

Stage 2
Understanding of
Cause-and-Effect Appears

CAUSE/
IN

Self

EFFECT/
KA

Visible Reality
Company-Employee
Hospital-Patient
School-Student

Stage 3
Understanding of In-En-Kahoh
Appears

Environment

CONDITIONS/
EN

CAUSE/
IN

Self

RESULT/
KAHOH

Visible Reality
Company-Employee
Hospital-Patient
School-Student

Figure 20 : The Stages in Understanding In-En-Kahoh

In-En-Kahoh (Inner Cause-Environmental Conditions-Result) in the Grand Challenge

The concept of **In-En-Kahoh** gives us a new way to understand the world for those of us engaged in the **Grand Challenge**, for where there are inner cause (**In**) and environmental conditions (**En**), there is always a result (**Kahoh**) and vice versa. Let us examine each part of this concept in greater detail (see Figure 21).

In (Inner Cause)

In refers to our human mind, attitudes, and thoughts. Our mind is composed, on the one hand, of our intentions, wishes, and motivations. On the other hand, it is also our **immediate feelings, perceptions, thoughts, and actions**. Our inner mind as a whole consists of "body, speech, and mind" or our attitudes, words, and thoughts.

En (Environmental Conditions)

In contrast to **In**, **En** is the set of environmental conditions that surround us. Although we exist because of a large variety of conditions, broadly speaking, they can be distilled into the following three. Within the larger environment that sustains us, the first element is **partners in the Way**. These are people close to us who understand our particular hopes and regrets. They are people we trust and walk on the path together with. The second condition is the **principles** that guide our lives. They might be legal regulations or unspoken rules, whether at school or work. And the third element is the **systems** or established procedures operating in our lives, both large and small.

To establish **En** or the environmental conditions that shape our lives, we must gather together with our **partners in the Way** and establish **principles** and **systems** to guide us.

Kahoh (Result)

Kahoh (results), both good and bad, come from the interaction of **In** and **En**. These results which appear as reality to us are sometimes built up over long periods of time and might seem hard to change. But it is important to remember that just as inner cause (**In**) and environmental conditions (**En**) produce results (**Kahoh**), all results or realities (**Kahoh**) must have arisen from both inner cause (**In**) and environ-

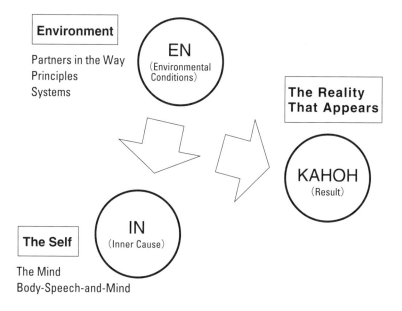

Figure 21 : In-En-Kahoh in the Grand Challenge

mental conditions (**En**). Therefore our inner self is reflected in the outer world because our inner cause (**In**) via the environmental conditions (**En**) forms and is formed by the outer reality (**Kahoh**).

Thus our approach to transforming a negative reality into a positive one is not to try to change the external circumstances, but rather, to return and change our inner cause (**In**) and environmental conditions (**En**) to a more positive direction, which will then naturally change the outer reality (result or **Kahoh**) as well. This is the fundamental attitude for engaging in the **Grand Challenge**.

We Cannot Change Results, But Can Change Cause-and-Conditions

When we don't realize that the **mind-and-form unit** consists of the interaction of our inner selves and the outer world, problems appear to us simply as external realities. Instead of changing the inner cause and environmental conditions (**In-En**) that gave rise to a problem, we stubbornly insist on trying to change the external result (**Kahoh**) alone. But it is virtually impossible to change the resultant external reality because we don't have authority over external reality. What we do have authority over is our own minds.

In a contradictory way, then, we try furiously to change the outer world, over which we have no authority, while ignoring the inner world where we have some control. Especially living in the complex world that we do, we find ourselves trying to tackle problems from all sorts of angles except the one that will actually effect a clear outcome. In other words, while we cannot change results (**Kahoh**), we have the ability to transform the inner cause and environmental conditions (**In-En**) that make up results.

Using this internal approach, when we come into conflict with someone, we can start by fully accepting the situation and inquire what this conflict asks of us. Instead of trying to figure out how to change the other person, we can look within ourselves to see how we can attend to the situation differently. Thus instead of changing the "result" (the other person) so as to "erase the problem," we must start by asking what needs to be changed at the **In**-level (within ourselves) and **En**-level (factors in our immediate environment). It is in this way that we can start to affect the **Kahoh** or result, slowly but surely. We must start by changing where we can actually make changes. **To look**

within ourselves and **to connect our inner selves and the outer world** is the time-tested true way to solve problems.

From a 20th- to 21st-Century Embodiment of Reality

The **20th-century approach to problem-solving**, which ignores the **In-En-Kahoh** system, has been to tackle problems head on by trying to turn negative realities into a positive direction directly. However, this approach soon reveals its limits and the fundamental problem is not solved. In the 20th-century model (see Figure 22), it is as if there always exists a huge barrier that cannot be crossed over between us and a positive solution, or even if we succeed in bridging the chasm, we distort the positive reality to a great extent because of our struggles with the barrier. This is clearly the model described above as the one that ignores the inner world while focusing solely on the outer world to solve problems.

In contrast, the **21st-century approach to problem-solving**, as found in the Grand Challenge and based on the wisdom of the **In-En-Kahoh**, doesn't try to alleviate situations by simply looking at the result. Rather, based on the principles of **to look within ourselves** and **to connect our inner selves and the outer world**, it advocates a three-step approach to changing problems from where they can actually be changed (see Figure 23).

Step 1 : Discovering the In-En-Kahoh (Inner Cause-Environmental Conditions-Result) of Negative Realities

The first step to solving problems is to view negative realities as a result (**Kahoh**) of inner cause and environmental conditions (**In-En**) that can be found within. Connecting our inner selves and the outer world like this, we can search for the real basis for the appearance of negative realities.

Step 2 : Transforming the In-En (Inner Cause and Environmental Conditions)

The power **to look within ourselves** allows us to transform the inner cause (our mind, **In**) of negative realities. Since our inner mind consists of our attitudes, words, and thoughts, we can start by adopting new attitudes, words, and thoughts. Furthermore, we can transform environmental conditions (the environment, **En**) with the help of sympathetic **partners in the Way** and put in place new **systems** realizing the **principles** governing the environment around us.

Step 3 : Creating the In-En-Kahoh (Inner Cause-Environmental Conditions-Result) of Positive Realities

The third step is a natural process in which more positive results (**Kahoh**) start appearing because of new inner cause and environmental conditions (**In-En**) that were developed in steps one and two.

Thus if we compare the 20th- and 21st-century approaches to problem-solving (see Figures 22 and 23 again), we can see that the **Grand Challenge** provides us with a bridge to cross over from negative to positive realities. This bridge allows us to finally be in touch with and resonate with the **six forces** of the universe. These **six forces**, which appear as **chaos** to us, can turn easily toward a negative reality because of the **four blades** that are embodied within our minds which interact with the chaotic reality. However, this very same **chaos** embodies the possibility of turning into a positive reality if we transform inner cause and environmental conditions (**In-En**) within ourselves.

Not taken by external realities, but rather focusing within and connecting our inner selves and the outer world, we can slowly but surely create a positive reality that is realized in **resonance with the six forces** of the universe which brings forth the new results. These are the principles to create the 21st century. Each small step we take, however minuscule it may seem, is truly the first step to creating a new world, the new millennium made present.

Records of the Grand Challenge

Here we will take up cases of two entrepreneurs who have attempted to bring about the new positive realities of the **Grand Challenge**.

A Record of an Individual's Grand Challenge XII
The Transformation of Kahoh
Ryoji Kawada, age 60, is the president of a machine-tool company having 50 employees in Nagoya City. Mr. Kawada has been studiously

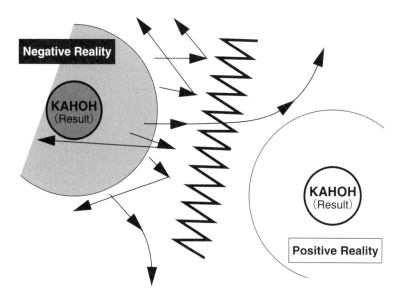

Figure 22 : The 20th-Century Approach to Problem-Solving

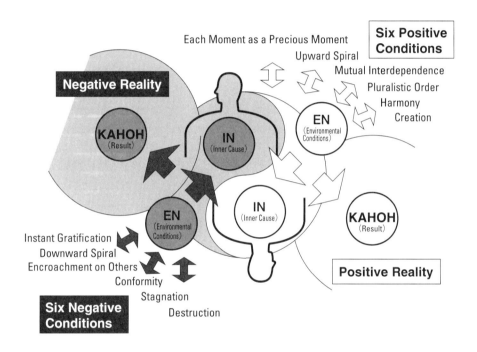

Figure 23 : The 21st-Century Approach to Problem-Solving

engaged in the various practices associated with the **Grand Challenge**. Over the years, he has clearly been able to transform negative realities, both at work and at home, into positive ones. Here, we will focus on how these transformations have changed his position as an entrepreneur. So that I could examine his life as an entrepreneur, he provided me with over 100 pieces of information (see Chart 20) about his situation at work (since his list included information about other companies or trade secrets, several items have been marked "----" to indicate responses which would not be appropriate to reveal here).

While becoming self-aware of one's situation is an important first step, simply laying out this information is only to outline **chaos** and doesn't serve as an analysis of it yet. However, when I reorganized his information into inner cause (**In**), environmental conditions (**En**), and result (**Kahoh**) (as it is in Charts 21-22) in terms of his positive and negative realities, it was possible to come up with the sequence of events in his transformation (see Figure 24). For example, in his original list, items 18/2-18/4 (see Chart 20 again) listed several statements which showed how Mr. Kawada thought that he was the most important person in the company. Therefore, I lumped those items together as a1 "I Am the Most Important Person in the World" (see Chart 21).

When a transformation takes place, very often one can go from one category to another. Therefore, in Mr. Kawada's case, his self-centered attitude (as a negative reality) appeared in its opposite form as "Respecting and Honoring the Employees" when he created a positive work reality (see Chart 22). Whenever possible, I have categorized these opposites with the same numbering system (small or capital letters); for example, in this case, "I Am the Most Important Person in the World" appears as a1, while "Respecting and Honoring the Employees" appears as A1.

Now let us turn to the overall transformation that occurred at Mr. Kawada's company. First, we can notice that there was a shift in his employees' attitudes and an improvement in company earnings. This is clear when we look at **Kahoh** (results), comparing the negative (c1 "Stagnation of Employee Morale" and c10 "Fragile Profits") with the positive (C1 "Increase in Employee Morale" and C10 "Improvement of Company Profits"). During the time when the negative reality was dominant, Mr. Kawada's company had just gone through the elimination of a failed division and three consecutive years in the red. This had led to the rebellion of an executive director and the resignation of major members of the sales team. His company was in serious trouble both within and without.

The Transformation of In

So how was such a transformation possible? The results didn't suddenly or directly go from negative to positive, but required changes within the minds of people before external results could show positive improvement. Mr. Kawada's own personal transformation, that is, changes in his **In** or inner cause, led to the transformation of his company. Mr. Kawada, when analyzed from the perspective of the **four personality types** discussed in Chapter 3, was clearly an **Over-Confident** type based on **Pleasure-Recklessness**, an orientation that he seemingly could do nothing about. But with the help of the **Reflections and Insight Sheet**, he was able to stop and look deeply into his mind to understand himself, in other words, his **immediate feelings**, **perceptions**, **thoughts and actions**. Furthermore, he was able, through this process, to see how his inner orientations shaped his external realities. Slowly but surely, making changes within resulted in changes without.

Mr. Kawada's **In** (inner cause) or mind, while shaped by negative forces, was characterized by a1 "I Am the Most Important Person in the World," a2 "Relationships Based on Rejection," and a3 "Self-Centered Relationships." Using the Sheets, he was able to see his **immediate feelings**, **perceptions**, **thoughts, and actions** and was thus able to turn toward a more positive self. His transformation was clear when we look at his positive **In**, A1 "Respecting and Honoring the Employees," A2 "Accepting Relationships," and A3 "Devoted Relationships." While he used to be a president who would expect all of his employees to come to him with requests or problems, he now is known to be a president who takes the initiative in knowing what is going on in every section of the company.

The Transformation of En

Furthermore, transformation occurred in the environmental conditions (**En**) that surrounded Mr. Kawada. These conditions (which include

00. The opening of the Vision 45 Program. A wonderful opportunity to see the brilliance of each employee.
01. Managers of each sales office seem to have a weak understanding of their position.
02. The president doesn't seem to understand trends among his customers.
03. Haven't been successful in gaining new clients.
04. Information on customers hasn't been systematically collected.
05. Employees don't reveal their weak points to the president.
06. The president explodes when he hears of mistakes by others.
07. ----
08. ----
09. Topics discussed are superficial because the sales meetings are only two-hour long.
10. Even after sales meetings, people repeat the same things and nothing seems to get better.
11. Sales meetings don't include careful deliberations.
12. Sales meetings only focus on short-term, immediate issues.
13. Meetings only focus on good news and bad news is avoided at all costs.
14. Because of his low sales, Department Director "A" keeps to himself.
15. Department Director "A" keeps quiet because he fears what others will say at the meetings.
16. ----
17. ----
18. The president is too obsessed with short-term profit.
18/2. The president thinks his employees will follow all his orders.
18/3. The president becomes unable to think objectively when faced with a problem.
18/4. The president issues order even though he may not be objective.
19.   ----
20. Sales Office Manager "D" comes to sales meetings but doesn't understand the reality of his office.
21. The older employees are still stuck with the idea of meeting quotas.
22. Though we've changed the meetings so that we have a rotating chairman, things haven't changed for the better.
23. Sales office managers give priority to their own office matters over the sales meetings.
24. Information from the sales meetings is not trickling down fully to all the employees.
25. Sales office managers only think about their own offices and lack the ability to think about the company as a whole.
26. Sales directions have not been transmitted to all the employees.
27. Employees' understanding of the company's sales directions is still weak.
28. The president hasn't been able to make a monthly visit to each sales office.
29. ---
30. The male employees at the Nagoya City sales

office don't greet each other properly in the morning.
31. The filing system at the Nagoya City sales office is unsystematic.
32. The employees at the Nagoya City sales office don't have a full understanding of corporate policy.
33. The employees at the Nagoya City sales office have difficulty looking within themselves when problems arise.
34. The female employees at the Nagoya City sales office have only passively accepted the Vision 45 Program.
35. There is a sales office which has been slow in setting up the LAN computer system.
36. There is a gap between what the company had envisioned and the LAN computer system we have adopted.
37. ----
38. The president hasn't decided who will take over the general affairs manager after he retired.
39. Employee "J" of the Nagoya City sales office was involved in a car accident while visiting a client.
40 - 43. ----
44. The president doesn't know the backgrounds of each employee very well.
45. The self-capital ratio of the 45th end-of-year account is low.
46. PR of new products is lacking. We have our hands full just with our established products.
47. Our company sales exist simply because of our brand name, Kawada.
48. Their is a big range in the results of the sales managers.
49. There's a need to continue the sales meetings more regularly.
50. Since there's no annual calendar for our meetings, it is hard to schedule meetings within our other operations.
51. The drill holder sold through the Tokyo sales office has not been selling and we are overstocked with them.
52. The printing equipment that was to have been sold through the Tokyo sales office has been behind schedule.
53. Since there is only one staff person at the Tokyo sales office and because of the trouble with the printing equipment, other clients have not been served from that office.
54. ----
55. The Tokyo sales office is messy.
56. ----
57. Employees are having to listen to one-way speeches by Assistant Director "C."
58. Assistant Director "C" has not been able to communicate sufficiently with others in his section.
59. Assistant Director "C" has a lack of understanding that his section is in charge of overall procurement.
60. Employee education has not been regular nor systematized.
61. Sales Office Manager "D" was in a traffic

Chart 20 : Mr. Kawada's Reality (as Described by Him)

accident while on holiday.

62. Sales Office Manager "K" was in a traffic accident in the early morning while on holiday.

63. The president has been able to assume leadership.

64. What the president does and says at home has begun to come together.

65. The president has started to accept what his employees say to him.

66. The president has started to look within himself when problems arise rather than look for external causes as before.

67. The president has stopped getting angry at the mistakes of others.

68. The president has started to take care of his health.

69. The president went to the year-end party for the first time.

70. The president has stopped drinking too much at social events and parties.

71. Department Director "A" has started to speak up.

72. Department Director "A" has begun to be able to see the problems of the company as a whole.

73. The sales meetings have started to develop a purpose.

74. The sales meetings have started to use an overhead projector.

75. The sales meetings have become a place to exchange information.

76. Each sales office has now set up a computer network.

77. A new employment system has been in place since October.

78. A new sales headquarter office was set up in an effort to centralize sales.

79. The sales department has been divided into two, which has made life easier for Department Director "F."

80. The rotating chairman system at the sales meeting has brought forth more energy for the participants.

81. Since September, Mr. "B" was promoted to executive director.

82. Executive Director "B" participated in a Total Life Human Principles Seminar.

83. Executive Director "B" will participate in a Grand Challenge Series Seminar.

84. The female employees at the Nagoya City sales office have started to make days with a "0" in them days to clean their offices.

85. The male employees at the Nagoya City sales office have started to take turns to clean the toilet.

86. The desk of the employee in charge of DH has been particularly tidy.

87. The meetings between the salesperson and the assistant at the Toyota City sales office have improved.

88. The Nagoya City sales office has asked the president to participate in their sales meetings.

89. Employees have been able to express their opinions more freely to the president.

90. Chief Clerk "H" has started to participate in meetings in the place of General Affairs Manager "G."

91. Employees have started to send information by FAX to the president's home.

92. Everyone at the Nagoya City sales office has begun learning how to use computers.

93. The daily report and other reports have begun to be produced from computer word processing.

94. Employees have eagerly embraced the introduction of the LAN computer system.

95. After the Vision 45 Program meeting, Executive Director "B" has started to view the employees as go-getters.

96. Employee morale has risen ever since the Vision 45 Program meeting.

97. Employees at the Toyota City sales office have become much cheerful ever since the Vision 45 Program meeting.

98. Employees at the Nagoya City sales office have begun twice-monthly Vision 45 Program meetings.

99. Employees have become invigorated ever since the Vision 45 Program meeting.

100. Manager "E" from the Tokyo sales office received many helpful hints from attending the Vision 45 Program meeting.

101. Our study group has become increasingly aware of its role in helping the president do his job.

102. There were no missed deadlines in providing conveyor belts to UIT Corporation.

103. We were able to help outfit UIT Corporation with design software.

104. We were able to negotiate a 50 percent cash payment plan with UIT Corporation.

105. Our profits have been the highest in six years.

106. The banks told us that our end-of-the-year accounts were unusually good.

107. The financial situation (cash flow) has improved.

108. We've been able to give out the highest bonuses in the past six years.

109. We were able to give out our bonuses as scheduled.

110. ----

111. The president's wife has been able to put her seal on documents after going over them.

112. The president's wife has started to participate in sales meetings as a board member.

113. The president's wife has been able to understand the meaning and purpose of meetings.

114. The president's wife has been able to more freely speak her mind to the president.

115. 116. ----

117. Sales Office Manager "E" from the Tokyo sales office set up a meeting to improve the assembly line of the printing system.

118. N Steel Corporation told us that the drill holders which we sold to them had been requested by two other companies.

Negative Reality

In (Inner Cause)

a1. "I Am the Most Important Person in the World"
18/2. The president thinks his employees will follow all his orders.

18/3. The president becomes unable to think objectively when faced with a problem.

18/4. The president issues order even though he may not be objective.

a2. Relationships Based on Rejection
06. The president explodes when he hears of mistakes by others.

a3. Self-Centered Relationships
02. The president doesn't seem to understand trends among his customers.

28. The president hasn't been able to make a monthly visit to each sales office.

44. The president doesn't know the backgrounds of each employee very well.

a4. Profit-Making Ideology
18. The president is too obsessed with short-term profit.

a5. Postponing Dealing with Problems
38. The president hasn't decided who will take over the general affairs manager after he retired.

En (Environmental Conditions)

b1. Department Director "A"
14. Because of his low sales, Department Director "A" keeps to himself.

15. Department Director "A" keeps quiet because he fears what others will say at the meetings.

b2.-b5. ----
07, 16, 17, 29, 40, 41, 42, 43, 54, 56, ----

b6. Sales Office Manager "D"
20. Sales Office Manager "D" comes to sales meetings but doesn't understand the reality of his office.

b7. Assistant Director "C"
58. Assistant Director "C" has not been able to communicate sufficiently with others in his section.

59. Assistant Director "C" has a lack of understanding that his section is in charge of overall procurement.

b8. The Unproductive Sales Meetings
09. Topics discussed are superficial because the sales meetings are only two-hour long.

11. Sales meetings don't include careful deliberations.

12. Sales meetings only focus on short-term, immediate issues.

13. Meetings only focus on good news and bad news is avoided at all costs.

22. Though we've changed the meetings so that we have a rotating chairman, things haven't changed for the better.

48. Their is a big range in the results of the sales managers.

49. There's a need to continue the sales meetings more regularly.

50. Since there's no annual calendar for our meetings, it is hard to schedule meetings within our other operations.

b9. Unproductive Information Systems
04. Information on customers hasn't been systematically collected.

31. The filing system at the Nagoya City sales office is unsystematic.

b10. Lack of Employee Education
60. Employee education has not been regular nor systematized.

Kahoh (Result)

c1. Stagnation of Employee Morale
30. The male employees at the Nagoya City sales office don't greet each other properly in the morning.

34. The female employees at the Nagoya City sales office have only passively accepted the Vision 45 Program.

c2. Lack of Listening
05. Employees don't reveal their weak points to the president.

57. Employees are having to listen to one-way speeches by Assistant Director "C."

(20.) Sales Office Manager "D" comes to sales meetings but doesn't understand the reality of his office.

Chart 21 : Mr. Kawada's Negative Reality Categorized

(54.) ----

(58.) Assistant Director "C" has not been able to communicate sufficiently with others in his section.

c3. Lack of Speaking Out

08. ----

10. Even after sales meetings, people repeat the same things and nothing seems to get better.

24. Information from the sales meetings is not trickling down fully to all the employees.

26. Sales directions have not been transmitted to all the employees.

27. Employees' understanding of the company's sales directions is still weak.

c4. Bad Timing

35. There is a sales office which has been slow in setting up the LAN computer system.

36. There is a gap between what the company had envisioned and the LAN computer system we have adopted.

51. The drill holder sold through the Tokyo sales office has not been selling and we are overstocked with them.

52. The printing equipment that was to have been sold through the Tokyo sales office has been behind schedule.

c5. Inability to Procure New Clients

03. Haven't been successful in gaining new clients.

46. PR of new products is lacking. We have our hands full just with our established products.

47. Our company sales exist simply because of our brand name, Kawada.

53. Since there is only one staff person at the Tokyo sales office and because of the trouble with the printing equipment, other clients have not been served from that office.

55. The Tokyo sales office is messy.

c6. Focus Only on Quotas

21. The older employees are still stuck with the idea of meeting quotas.

(07.) ----

(14.) Because of his low sales, Department Director "A" keeps to himself.

c7. Sales Office Managers Look Out Only for Themselves

01. Managers of each sales office seem to have a weak understanding of their position.

23. Sales office managers give priority to their own office matters over the sales meetings.

25. Sales office managers only think about their own offices and lack the ability to think about the company as a whole.

c8. Lack of Understanding of Corporate Policy

32. The employees at the Nagoya City sales office don't have a full understanding of corporate policy.

33. The employees at the Nagoya City sales office have difficulty looking within themselves when problems arise.

c9. Traffic Accidents

39. Employee "J" of the Nagoya City sales office was involved in a car accident while visiting a client.

61. Sales Office Manager "D" was in a traffic accident while on holiday.

62. Sales Office Manager "K" was in a traffic accident in the early morning while on holiday.

c10. Fragile Profits

45. The self-capital ratio of the 45th end-of-year account is low.

Positive Reality

In (Inner Cause)
A1. Respecting and Honoring the Employees
00. The opening of the Vision 45 Program. A wonderful opportunity to see the brilliance of each employee.

A2. Accepting Relationships
65. The president has started to accept what his employees say to him.
66. The president has started to look within himself when problems arise rather than look for external causes as before.
67. The president has stopped getting angry at the mistakes of others.

A3. Devoted Relationships
63. The president has been able to assume leadership.
64. What the president does and says at home has begun to come together.
68. The president has started to take care of his health.
69. The president went to the year-end party for the first time.
70. The president has stopped drinking too much at social events and parties.

En (Environmental Conditions)
B1. Department Director "A"
71. Department Director "A" has started to speak up.
72. Department Director "A" has begun to be able to see the problems of the company as a whole.

B2. Executive Director "B"
81. Since September, Mr. "B" was promoted to executive director.
82. Executive Director "B" participated in a Total Life Human Principles Seminar.
83. Executive Director "B" will participate in a Grand Challenge Series Seminar.
95. After the Vision 45 Program meeting, Executive Director "B" has started to view the employees as go-getters.

B3. Sales Office Manager "E"
100. Manager "E" from the Tokyo sales office received many helpful hints from attending the Vision 45 Program meeting.

B4. The President's Cooperation with His Wife
111. The president's wife has been able to put her seal on documents after going over them.
112. The president's wife has started to participate in sales meetings as a board member.
113. The president's wife has been able to understand the meaning and purpose of meetings.
114. The president's wife has been able to more freely speak her mind to the president.

B8. More Productive Sales Meeting
73. The sales meetings have started to develop a purpose.
74. The sales meetings have started to use an overhead projector.
75. The sales meetings have become a place to exchange information.
80. The rotating chairman system at the sales meeting has brought forth more energy for the participants.

B9. More Productive Information System
76. Each sales office has now set up a computer network.

B11. A More Active Study Group
101. Our study group has become increasingly aware of its role in helping the president do his job.

B12. Transformation in the Organization
77. A new employment system has been in place since October.
78. A new sales headquarter office was set up in an effort to centralize sales.
79. The sales department has been divided into two, which has made life easier for Department Director "F."
90. Chief Clerk "H" has started to participate in meetings in the place of General Affairs Manager "G."

Kahoh (Result)
C1. Increase in Employee Morale
84. The female employees at the Nagoya City sales office have started to make days with a "0" in them days to clean their offices.
85. The male employees at the Nagoya City sales

Chart 22: Mr. Kawada's Positive Reality Categorized

office have started to take turns to clean the toilet.

86. The desk of the employee in charge of DH has been particularly tidy.

92. Everyone at the Nagoya City sales office has begun learning how to use computers.

93. The daily report and other reports have begun to be produced from computer word processing.

94. Employees have eagerly embraced the introduction of the LAN computer system.

96. Employee morale has risen ever since the Vision 45 Program meeting.

97. Employees at the Toyota City sales office have become much cheerful ever since the Vision 45 Program meeting.

98. Employees at the Nagoya City sales office have begun twice-monthly Vision 45 Program meetings.

99. Employees have become invigorated ever since the Vision 45 Program meeting.

C2. Better Listening

87. The meetings between the salesperson and the assistant at the Toyota City sales office have improved.

88. The Nagoya City sales office has asked the president to participate in their sales meetings.

89. Employees have been able to express their opinions more freely to the president.

91. Employees have started to send information by FAX to the president's home.

C4. Better Response

102. There were no missed deadlines in providing conveyor belts to UIT Corporation.

103. We were able to help outfit UIT Corporation with design software.

104. We were able to negotiate a 50 percent cash payment plan with UIT Corporation.

C5. Procurement of New Clients

117. Sales Office Manager "E" from the Tokyo sales office set up a meeting to improve the assembly line of the printing system.

118. N Steel Corporation told us that the drill holders which we sold to them had been requested by two other companies.

C10. Improvement of Company Profits

105. Our profits have been the highest in six years.

106. The banks told us that our end-of-the-year accounts were unusually good.

107. The financial situation (cash flow) has improved.

108. We've been able to give out the highest bonuses in the past six years.

109. We were able to give out our bonuses as scheduled.

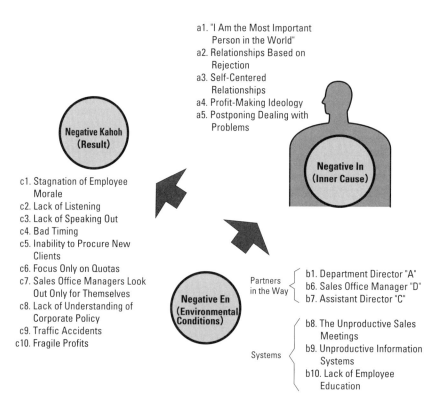

a1. "I Am the Most Important Person in the World"
a2. Relationships Based on Rejection
a3. Self-Centered Relationships
a4. Profit-Making Ideology
a5. Postponing Dealing with Problems

Negative Kahoh (Result)

Negative In (Inner Cause)

c1. Stagnation of Employee Morale
c2. Lack of Listening
c3. Lack of Speaking Out
c4. Bad Timing
c5. Inability to Procure New Clients
c6. Focus Only on Quotas
c7. Sales Office Managers Look Out Only for Themselves
c8. Lack of Understanding of Corporate Policy
c9. Traffic Accidents
c10. Fragile Profits

Negative En (Environmental Conditions)

Partners in the Way
b1. Department Director "A"
b6. Sales Office Manager "D"
b7. Assistant Director "C"

Systems
b8. The Unproductive Sales Meetings
b9. Unproductive Information Systems
b10. Lack of Employee Education

Figure 24 : Mr. Kawada's Negative and Positive In-En-Kahoh

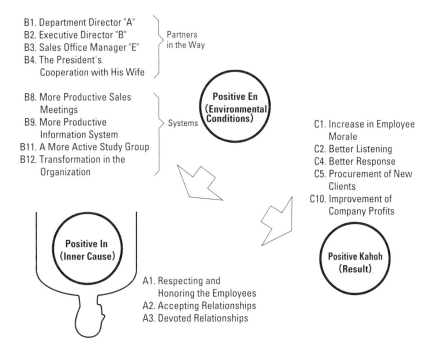

B1. Department Director "A"
B2. Executive Director "B"
B3. Sales Office Manager "E"
B4. The President's
     Cooperation with His Wife

Partners
in the Way

B8. More Productive Sales
     Meetings
B9. More Productive
     Information System
B11. A More Active Study Group
B12. Transformation in the
     Organization

Systems

Positive En
(Environmental
Conditions)

C1. Increase in Employee
     Morale
C2. Better Listening
C4. Better Response
C5. Procurement of New
     Clients
C10. Improvement of
     Company Profits

Positive In
(Inner Cause)

Positive Kahoh
(Result)

A1. Respecting and
     Honoring the Employees
A2. Accepting Relationships
A3. Devoted Relationships

human **partners in the Way**, **principles**, and **systems**), in the case of Mr. Kawada's company, fell into two types: partners in the Way and systems. In terms of human relationships, one can clearly see the transformation from the negative to the positive, especially in terms of b1, Department Director "A." While this department director used to keep to himself because he feared what others would say at the meetings because of his low sales volume, he joined Mr. Kawada as a **partner in the Way** through study group meetings. Learning to feel included among the other executives in the company, he showed a marked improvement toward a more positive reality (see B1, "has started to speak up" and "has begun to be able to see the problems of the company as a whole"). Other people affected by Mr. Kawada's transformation included Executive Director "B" (B2) and his wife (B4).

But it was not only people (**partners in the Way**), but whole **systems** at the company that were affected by Mr. Kawada's inner change. We can see the vast difference at what occurred at sales meetings in terms of employee involvement and productivity of the meetings (see b8 and B8).

The Transformation of In-En-Kahoh

The final results (**Kahoh**) in terms of the company's profits and employees' satisfaction at work were also dramatic. This process was not a random one, but involved stopping the negative pattern of thinking and behavior as well as a turn toward the positive. For example, when we look at the transition from c2 to C2, we can see the shift from a hierarchical company to one where people listened to each other. In all the transitions from "c" to "C," however, what is important to note is the fact that they all began with an inner transformation within Mr. Kawada which spread outward.

Resonating with the Six Forces

In going through this process, Mr. Kawada was able to access the **six forces** (**flow**, **linkage**, **circulation**, **balance**, **creation**, **eruption**) and turn them toward a more positive reality. In terms of **flow** and **linkage** for example, while the employees had previously only thought of their limited area, gradually they came to understand how they were mutually interdependent and precious, getting involved in a much more energetic and intimate way with the affairs of the company as a whole. In many other ways, this transformation thus involved not only a transition from a negative to a positive pattern of thought and behavior, but an orientation of the **six forces** toward the light. This is the true meaning of **resonating with the universe**.

A Record of an Individual's Grand Challenge XIII

In Chapter 4, we took up the case of Hisao Kinouchi, age 47, in the Kansai region of Japan. He is the president of a major industrial materials supplier, which had been a family-run business for over 200 years. For this exercise, I asked him to write out a list of items regarding the situation at his company, past and present. He came up with a list of 182 items which he divided into positive and negative realities at the firm (Charts 23-24). As with Mr. Kawada, I categorized Mr. Kinouchi's list into negative and positive **In-En-Kahoh** (see Charts 25-26).

The transformations from the negative to positive realities for Mr. Kinouchi and his company (see Figure 25) must also be placed in the context of what I call the teachings of "wisdom." What is meant by **wisdom** is the ability to cross over from the shore of suffering to the shore of liberation, as if placing a bridge from a riverbank to islands in-between (see Chapter 4 of my book, *Discovery*, for more on this). This process is the Buddhist path described as 1) knowing the reality or present situation (suffering), 2) seeing into the causes (causes of suffering), 3) making sure of the purpose or vision of the future (the elimination of the causes of suffering) and setting up the goals, and finally 4) making the method for reaching there (the Path) clear (see Figure 26).

Liberation, however, can take a much more specific character. In Mr. Kinouchi's case, the process of his journey was to fulfill the purposes of a) a community bound together and b) a vibrant, profitable company. The sense of community that he so wished for stemmed from the fact that his firm had a 200-year-old tradition with employees both young and old. His was a hope and vision that they could all be bound together in a common purpose. This life-long concern with community-building was also connected to another hope of his: growth of the company. Partly because of its long history, the company had accomplished a certain level of stability. However, this stability had led

Negative Reality

01. Sales have been stagnant for three consecutive years.
02. ----
03. My father's hearing has deteriorated and it has become hard to communicate with him.
04. When Executive Director "A" is in a bad mood, it is very apparent. The atmosphere at the company as a whole becomes sour.
05. ----
06. Executive Director "A" seems to be driven solely by self-benefit.
07. Good client procurement in the Kanto region, which had come from the efforts of 20 years, has steeply declined in the last three years.
08. Products that sold well in the Kanto region are not doing well these days.
09. Can't stop thinking about the loss of clients in the Kanto region, which was an area that I had a major hand in.
10. Products that we created in the past haven't sold well recently because of competition from other companies and the current recession.
11. There haven't been any hit products from our suppliers.
12. Having put an emphasis on accounting and finances recently, I have been drawn away from the realities of sales.
13. ----
14. ----
15. There have been many complaints regarding our forestry-related products.
16. Our new products haven't been catching fire.
17. We don't have any leaders in the agro-forestry machine products department.
18. We haven't cleared up sales methods in the agro-forestry machine products department.
19. The review committee in the agro-forestry machine products department hasn't shown any results.
20. Sales per person in the agro-forestry machine products department is low compared to other departments.
21. There has been a loss in demand from construction-related industries.
22. The young salesman "J" in the agro-forestry machine products department was unable to fully meet the requests of a customer.
23. ----
24. Was told by a client that we need to provide products that better fit their overall project plan.
25. Manager "N" from the industrial supplies division 1 lacks overall vision and leadership.
26. Manager "P" from the industrial supplies division 2 lacks a cooperative attitude and everyone gets tense.
27. Worried about the life style (especially finances) of Manager "O" from the industrial supplies division 2.
28. General Affairs Division Manager "I" lacks imagination and a sensibility to helping others.
29. The female staff don't answer the telephone appropriately.
30. Sales at stores are still low.
31. "G" in agro-forestry machine products department cannot take care of business scrupulously.
32. One of the salesmen clearly lacks drive.
33. The female staff's work has become routine.
34. ----
35. Mid-level managers have been complaining of the lack of access to the executive members of the company.
36. Our suppliers don't seem to be visiting us.
37. Executive Director "A" seems to be giving a bad impression to our suppliers. I can't help wondering how others view our company.
38. I'm still relying on my father.
39. Accounting has taken up so much of my time that I can't attend to sales.
40. I haven't been able to visit the distribution center very often.
41. Think I've gotten somewhere after a period of study.
42. Feel uncomfortable being a Total Life Human Principles Corporation when sales are low.
43. Wonder how others view me when I skip industry-wide conferences.
44. Always leave in the morning worrying about being late to work.
45. Chief Clerk "HB" has driven down the margins in a department that I started up. Can't help wondering why.
46. Don't see leadership qualities in one of the chief clerks.
47. Since I haven't been able to visit the distribution center much this past year, I've left everything up to Department Executive "B."
48. One of the newly hired employees at the distribution center quit in just over a month.

Chart 23 : Mr. Kinouchi's Negative Reality (as Described by Him)

49. Organization and cleanliness at the distribution center have been lacking.

50. Though the employees at the distribution center have a lot of potential, they don't put it to use by cooperating with each other.

51. Have been resigned to the loss of sales in the Kanto region.

52. The profit margin always seems to fall in the new products sector.

53. Get frustrated because work doesn't seem to get done.

54. Sometimes get worried about the lethargy of the company.

55. The president hasn't been able to sort through mail and company documents properly.

56. Can't see the future direction the company should be taking in the upcoming year.

57. ----

58. Get envious toward companies that are doing well.

59. My personal savings account is awfully low and this makes me feel ashamed.

60. Overwhelmed by the schedule, I sometimes give up.

61. ----

62. Often feel sleepy and slothful.

63. Wonder if it's really possible to put the Total Life Human Principles in action at my business during this time of recession.

64. Opportunities to visit customers have declined.

65. However hard I try, I can't compare with my father in terms of accounting.

66-71. ----

72. Feel sorry for my family when I am overwhelmed with work.

73. ----

74. The president's desk is messy.

75. Our company's products have a low technological level.

76. New products sent to our clients and retailers have lost their edge.

77. Small lots have increased.

78. When Executive Director "A" is in a bad mood, he quickly fights with our suppliers.

79. It gets hard to make things go smoothly if I don't share the same opinion as Executive Director "A."

80. Now that father is better, I feel that I don't need to make further efforts.

81. Even though I have been recommending the study groups to my father, he seems weak-hearted.

82. My wife has misunderstandings about the Total Life management system.

83. It has become hard to talk about the study group meetings to my wife.

84. Old and established sales patterns are hard to change.

85. My father cannot get away from a profit-driven and family-oriented business model.

86. My wife gets upset when I stay away from the house for too long.

87. I just wonder in amazement when I see untalented sales people.

88. On sales rounds, I've been told that my serious demeanor seems more suited for being a doctor or a lawyer than a salesman.

89. Chief Clerk "H" has not shown leadership qualities in the agro-forestry machine products department yet and thus relies on employee "G" too much.

90. The president's vision has not yet spread to the mid-level managers.

91. Salesman "L" has poor sales to retailers, but this fact is ignored.

Positive Reality

01. It's been five, healthy years since my father's operation.
02. Members of the company have been developing solid relationships with each other.
03. In the past three years, although five employees have retired, they have stayed on as directors or part-time employees.
04. Getting over past disagreements, I managed to develop a friendship with the former Executive Director.
05. The female employees have become more energetic and participatory in company-sponsored events.
06. Several male employees, who up till three years ago didn't participate in company-sponsored events, have all begun to.
07. We've had no major traffic or construction accidents in the past several years.
08. Executive Director "A" and Department Executive "B" have started to talk with me before the meetings or each time a problem arises.
09. The accounting department, which used to be run solely by my father, is now ably managed by the president, Department Executive "B," Manager "PB," and several female employees.
10. While accounting and all finance-related business used to be handled by the chairman of the Board, I have managed to handle this area by myself.
11. The financial situation is now stable and smoothly run.
12. Manager "PB," who used to be a poor performer in sales, has raised his performance in accounting with the aid of a computer.
13. When employees are in the midst of an important phase in their lives, I try to respond appropriately.
14. Manager "T," who has been working with Department Executive "B," has begun to recognize his tendency to order people around.
15. The female employees have emphasized friendliness.
16. I was able to convey my appreciation of the Total Life Human Principles to my wife.
17. My wife has become less of a stickler about my coming home late.
18. ----
19. Want to encourage local chapters of the Total Life Management.
20. Have been able to look within myself whenever I'm faced with crises.
21. Have been thinking more and more that I can get the job done.
22. Have been able to say "No" to things that I know are wrong.
23. Have been able to empty my mind when things start to bother me.
24. My daughter, who had been rebelling, has begun to warm up since last fall.
25. Began thinking that I want to be an exemplar of the Total Life Human Principles even though I don't amount to much.
26. Have been able to confide in my partners in the Way when work starts to pile up.
27. Living with my family has started to become fun.
28. Am happy when my employees do good work.
29. Have started to be able to cry whenever I see or come into contact with dramatic events, literature, sports, or music.
30. Have served on the staff of the Total Life Management for five years.
31. ----
32. Though there were several employees whose health has deteriorated, they are all well now.
33. The three new employees are all out-going and promising.
34. Tree planting has been born as a new activity at the company through the joint efforts of the president and the employees.
35. I made a presentation at the first Total Life Human Principles Seminar in Kyoto.
36. I made a presentation on Ms. Takahashi's book, Discovery, in Kyoto.
37. The net to prevent wildlife destruction, developed by the agro-forestry machine products department, has recently been adopted at the local forest services department.
38. Studying Ms. Takahashi's "wisdom" teachings has become a part of the pre-sales-meeting get together of the President, Executive Director "A," and the Department Executive "B."
39. Young employees have adopted the practice of serving in all seven divisions within the company.
40. Since 1996, the theme "A Community Bound Together" has been adopted by the employees with the goal of achieving it in the year 2001.
41. Under the supervision of Department

Chart 24 : Mr. Kinouchi's Positive Reality (as Described by Him)

Executive "B," the retail and facility installation business have increased to the level of the wholesale business of the company.

42. For ten years, our company has maintained a New Year's resolution presentation by the employees for the upcoming year's goals.

43. The executive directors and the lower-level managers have been able to communicate and discuss the company's agenda in pre-meeting and post-meeting get-togethers.

43/2. Though the oldest employee of the company, "F," has retired, he has continued in good spirits as a part-time employee at the store.

44. Though "G" has retired from the agro-forestry machine products department, he has continued to help out with the sales as a part-time employee.

45. Executive Director "A" has been increasingly mellow in these past few years.

46. Although a new client that Executive Director "A" had procured went bankrupt, thus inflicting financial loss on our company, I decided to take personal responsibility for the situation.

47. Manager "C," who has been working in the wholesale division for the past 30 years, has decided to take leadership at his division.

48. Manager "M," who has been working in the retail division for the past 29 years, has increased profits in the division and also begun thinking more about training those under his supervision.

49. Assistant Chief Clerk "H" of agro-forestry machine products department, when promoted to chief clerk, began working out supplier routes by himself.

50. Chief Clerk "R," who has been in charge of the tree planting project at the company, has taken over this division from the president even though it was hard hit in the post-bubble economy period.

51. Company employees as a whole have been guided by a yearly theme chosen by the president based on the Total Life Human Principles.

52. I have started to dedicate myself to the Total Life Human Principles and to pray for each employee.

53. The company has been able to maintain profits even in the post-bubble economy period.

54-82. ----

83. Manager "E"'s face has started to cheer up as he has begun looking after those under his supervision more.

84. The tree planting project, which has not been a profitable division, completed a major project in Shiga Prefecture this past spring.

85. Managers "D" and "E" have increased their per-unit sales.

86. I've been able to share my true feelings with my wife.

87. Through discussions with the president, Chief Clerk "H" of agro-forestry machine products department has begun conceiving of a project to restore damaged mountain forests.

88. Director "Q," under instructions from the president, has undertaken a project to invent a new product line.

89. Executive Director "A," who had previously taken no interest in the agro-forestry machine products department, has taken the lead in the new products development at that department.

90. My parents met Ms. Takahashi and came to understand why I have been studying the Total Life Human Principles.

Negative Reality

In (Inner Cause)

a1. Notions of Self-Importance and Hierarchy

06. Executive Director "A" seems to be driven solely by self-benefit.
27. Worried about the life style (especially finances) of Manager "O" from the industrial supplies division 2.
28. General Affairs Division Manager "I" lacks imagination and a sensibility to helping others.
45. Chief Clerk "HB" has driven down the margins in a department that I started up. Can't help wondering why.
59. My personal savings account is awfully low and this makes me feel ashamed.
87. I just wonder in amazement when I see untalented sales people.

a2. Dependent and Opportunistic Relationships

09. Can't stop thinking about the loss of clients in the Kanto region, which was an area that I had a major hand in.
37. Executive Director "A" seems to be giving a bad impression to our suppliers. I can't help wondering how others view our company.
38. I'm still relying on my father.
43. Wonder how others view me when I skip industry-wide conferences.
44. Always leave in the morning worrying about being late to work.
53. Get frustrated because work doesn't seem to get done.
65. However hard I try, I can't compare with my father in terms of accounting.
72. Feel sorry for my family when I am overwhelmed with work.
79. It gets hard to make things go smoothly if I don't share the same opinion as Executive Director "A."
83. It has become hard to talk about the study group meetings to my wife.

a3. Putting Distance between Himself and Others

18. We haven't cleared up sales methods in the agro-forestry machine products department.
47. Since I haven't been able to visit the distribution center much this past year, I've left everything up to Department Executive "B."
88. On sales rounds, I've been told that my serious demeanor seems more suited for being a doctor or a lawyer than a salesman.

a4. Conformity without Taking Risks

41. Think I've gotten somewhere after a period of study.
60. Overwhelmed by the schedule, I sometimes give up.
80. Now that father is better, I feel that I don't need to make further efforts.

a5. Lack of Ability to Sort Out Information

55. The president hasn't been able to sort through mail and company documents properly.
74. The president's desk is messy.

a6. Pressure Felt from a Lack of Profits

42. Feel uncomfortable being a Total Life Human Principles Corporation when sales are low.
58. Get envious toward companies that are doing well.

a7. Giving Up Trying to Change Reality

51. Have been resigned to the loss of sales in the Kanto region.
62. Often feel sleepy and slothful.

a8. Loneliness and Uncertainty

54. Sometimes get worried about the lethargy of the company.
56. Can't see the future direction the company should be taking in the upcoming year.
63. Wonder if it's really possible to put the Total Life Human Principles in action at my business during this time of recession.

En (Environmental Conditions)

b1. Parents (Father)

03. My father's hearing has deteriorated and it has become hard to communicate with him.
81. Even though I have been recommending the study groups to my father, he seems weak-hearted.
85. My father cannot get away from a profit-driven and family-oriented business model.

b2. Executive Director "A"

04. When Executive Director "A" is in a bad mood, it is very apparent. The atmosphere at the company as a whole becomes sour.
35. Mid-level managers have been complaining of the lack of access to the executive members of the company.
78. When Executive Director "A" is in a bad mood, he quickly fights with our suppliers.

b3. Wife

82. My wife has misunderstandings about the Total

Chart 25 : Mr. Kinouchi's Negative Reality Categorized

Life management system.

86. My wife gets upset when I stay away from the house for too long.

b4. Decline in the Value of the Products

08. Products that sold well in the Kanto region are not doing well these days.

10. Products that we created in the past haven't sold well recently because of competition from other companies and the current recession.

11. There haven't been any hit products from our suppliers.

24. Was told by a client that we need to provide products that better fit their overall project plan.

75. Our company's products have a low technological level.

76. New products sent to our clients and retailers have lost their edge.

b5. The Small Trickle of Information-Exchange with the Sales Department

12. Having put an emphasis on accounting and finances recently, I have been drawn away from the realities of sales.

39. Accounting has taken up so much of my time that I can't attend to sales.

40. I haven't been able to visit the distribution center very often.

64. Opportunities to visit customers have declined.

b6. The Inflexibility of Old Systems Continuing

15. There have been many complaints regarding our forestry-related products.

19. The review committee in the agro-forestry machine products department hasn't shown any results.

36. Our suppliers don't seem to be visiting us.

77. Small lots have increased.

52. The profit margin always seems to fall in the new products sector.

84. Old and established sales patterns are hard to change.

Kahoh (Result)
c1. Fragile Profits

01. Sales have been stagnant for three consecutive years.

07. Good client procurement in the Kanto region, which had come from the efforts of 20 years, has steeply declined in the last three years.

16. Our new products haven't been catching fire.

21. There has been a loss in demand from construction-related industries.

c2. Lack of Morale among Younger Employees

32. One of the salesmen clearly lacks drive.

46. Don't see leadership qualities in one of the chief clerks.

c3. Lack of Ability among the Salesmen

22. The young salesman "J" in the agro-forestry machine products department was unable to fully meet the requests of a customer.

91. Salesman "L" has poor sales to retailers, but this fact is ignored.

c4. Lack of Ability among Mid-Level Managers

25. Manager "N" from the industrial supplies division 1 lacks overall vision and leadership.

26. Manager "P" from the industrial supplies division 2 lacks a cooperative attitude and everyone gets tense.

31. "G" in agro-forestry machine products department cannot take care of business scrupulously.

89. Chief Clerk "H" has not shown leadership qualities in the agro-forestry machine products department yet and thus relies on employee "G" too much.

90. The president's vision has not yet spread to the mid-level managers.

c5. Lack of Ability among the Female Staff

29. The female staff don't answer the telephone appropriately.

33. The female staff's work has become routine.

34. ----

c6. Certain Divisions Falling Behind

17. We don't have any leaders in the agro-forestry machine products department.

20. Sales per person in the agro-forestry machine products department is low compared to other departments.

30. Sales at stores are still low.

c7. Disorganization at the Distribution Center

48. One of the newly hired employees at the distribution center quit in just over a month.

49. Organization and cleanliness at the distribution center have been lacking.

50. Though the employees at the distribution center have a lot of potential, they don't put it to use by cooperating with each other.

Positive Reality

In (Inner Cause)
A1. Certainty of the Truth
25. Began thinking that I want to be an exemplar of the Total Life Human Principles even though I don't amount to much.
16. I was able to convey my appreciation of the Total Life Human Principles to my wife.

A2. Prayers for His Employees
13. When employees are in the midst of an important phase in their lives, I try to respond appropriately.
28. Am happy when my employees do good work.
52. I have started to dedicate myself to the Total Life Human Principles and to pray for each employee.

A3. Increase in Self-Responsibility
10. While accounting and all finance-related business used to be handled by the chairman of the Board, I have managed to handle this area by myself.
19. Want to encourage local chapters of the Total Life Management.
21. Have been thinking more and more that I can get the job done.
35. I made a presentation at the first Total Life Human Principles Seminar in Kyoto.
36. I made a presentation on Ms. Takahashi's book, Discovery, in Kyoto.
46. Although a new client that Executive Director "A" had procured went bankrupt, thus inflicting financial loss on our company, I decided to take personal responsibility for the situation.

A4. Self-Discipline
(10.) While accounting and all finance-related business used to be handled by the chairman of the Board, I have managed to handle this area by myself.
20. Have been able to look within myself whenever I'm faced with crises.
22. Have been able to say "No" to things that I know are wrong.
23. Have been able to empty my mind when things start to bother me.

A5. Recovery of an Ability to Feel
29. Have started to be able to cry whenever I see or come into contact with dramatic events, literature, sports, or music.

En (Environmental Conditions)
B1. Parents
90. My parents met Ms. Takahashi and came to understand why I have been studying the Total Life Human Principles.
01. It's been five, healthy years since my father's operation.

B2. Better Relationships with Executive Directors
08. Executive Director "A" and Department Executive "B" have started to talk with me before the meetings or each time a problem arises.
(38.) Studying Ms. Takahashi's "wisdom" teachings has become a part of the pre-sales-meeting get-together of the President, Executive Director "A," and the Department Executive "B."
14. Manager "T," who has been working with Department Executive "B," has begun to recognize his tendency to order people around.
45. Executive Director "A" has been increasingly mellow in these past few years.

B3. Wife
17. My wife has become less of a stickler about my coming home late.
86. I've been able to share my true feelings with my wife.

B4. Partners in the Total Life Human Principles
26. Have been able to confide in my partners in the Way when work starts to pile up.
30. Have served on the staff of the Total Life Management for five years.

B5. The Greater Adoption of the Total Life Human Principles
15. The female employees have emphasized friendliness.
40. Since 1996, the theme "A Community Bound Together" has been adopted by the employees with the goal of achieving it in the year 2001.
42. For ten years, our company has maintained a New Year's resolution presentation by the employees for the upcoming year's goals.
51. Company employees as a whole have been guided by a yearly theme chosen by the president based on the Total Life Human Principles.

B6. The Reform of the Accounting System
09. The accounting department, which used to be run solely by my father, is now ably managed by the president, Department Executive "B," Manager "PB," and several female employees.
12. Manager "PB," who used to be a poor performer in sales, has raised his performance in accounting with the aid of a computer.

B7. The Organization of a System Which

Chart 26 : Mr. Kinouchi's Positive Reality Categorized

Nurtures the Younger Employees

39. Young employees have adopted the practice of serving in all seven divisions within the company.
43. The executive directors and the lower-level managers have been able to communicate and discuss the company's agenda in pre-meeting and post-meeting get-togethers.

B8. Cooperation to Develop New Products

34. Tree planting has been born as a new activity at the company through the joint efforts of the president and the employees.
41. Under the supervision of Department Executive "B," the retail and facility installation business have increased to the level of the wholesale business of the company.
87. Through discussions with the president, Chief Clerk "H" of agro-forestry machine products department has begun conceiving of a project to restore damaged mountain forests.
88. Director "Q," under instructions from the president, has undertaken a project to invent a new product line.
89. Executive Director "A," who had previously taken no interest in the agro-forestry machine products department, has taken the lead in the new products development at that department.

B9. The Wisdom Teachings at Sales Meetings

38. Studying Ms. Takahashi's "wisdom" teachings has become a part of the pre-sales-meeting get-together of the President, Executive Director "A," and the Department Executive "B."

Kahoh (Result)

C1. Stable Profits

11. The financial situation is now stable and smoothly run.
53. The company has been able to maintain profits even in the post-bubble economy period.

C2. Better Relationships

02. Members of the company have been developing solid relationships with each other.
05. The female employees have become more energetic and participatory in company-sponsored events.
06. Several male employees, who up till three years ago didn't participate in company-sponsored events, have all begun to.
33. The three new employees are all out-going and promising.
83. Manager "E"'s face has started to cheer up as he has begun looking after those under his supervision more.

C3. Better Relationships with Senior Employees

03. In the past three years, although five employees have retired, they have stayed on as directors or part-time employees.
04. Getting over past disagreements, I managed to develop a friendship with the former Executive Director.
43/2. Though the oldest employee of the company, "F," has retired, he has continued in good spirits as a part-time employee at the store.
44. Though "G" has retired from the agro-forestry machine products department, he has continued to help out with the sales as a part-time employee.

C4. Developments in New Projects

37. The net to prevent wildlife destruction, developed by the agro-forestry machine products department, has recently been adopted at the local forest services department.
84. The tree planting project, which has not been a profitable division, completed a major project in Shiga Prefecture this past spring.
85. Managers "D" and "E" have increased their per-unit sales.

C5. An Increase in the Consciousness of Mid-Level Managers

47. Manager "C," who has been working in the wholesale division for the past 30 years, has decided to take leadership at his division.
48. Manager "M," who has been working in the retail division for the past 29 years, has increased profits in the division and also begun thinking more about training those under his supervision.
49. Assistant Chief Clerk "H" of agro-forestry machine products department, when promoted to chief clerk, began working out supplier routes by himself.
50. Chief Clerk "R," who has been in charge of the tree planting project at the company, has taken over this division from the president even though it was hard hit in the post-bubble economy period.

C6. Good Health of Employees

07. We've had no major traffic or construction accidents in the past several years.
32. Though there were several employees whose health has deteriorated, they are all well now.

C7. Improvement in Family Relationships

24. My daughter, who had been rebelling, has begun to warm up since last fall.
27. Living with my family has started to become fun.

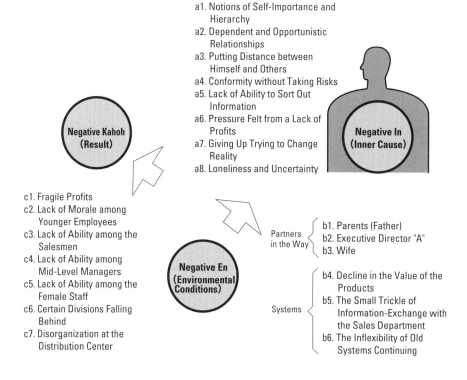

a1. Notions of Self-Importance and
    Hierarchy
a2. Dependent and Opportunistic
    Relationships
a3. Putting Distance between
    Himself and Others
a4. Conformity without Taking Risks
a5. Lack of Ability to Sort Out
    Information
a6. Pressure Felt from a Lack of
    Profits
a7. Giving Up Trying to Change
    Reality
a8. Loneliness and Uncertainty

Negative Kahoh
(Result)

Negative In
(Inner Cause)

c1. Fragile Profits
c2. Lack of Morale among
    Younger Employees
c3. Lack of Ability among the
    Salesmen
c4. Lack of Ability among
    Mid-Level Managers
c5. Lack of Ability among the
    Female Staff
c6. Certain Divisions Falling
    Behind
c7. Disorganization at the
    Distribution Center

Negative En
(Environmental
Conditions)

Partners
in the Way

b1. Parents (Father)
b2. Executive Director "A"
b3. Wife

Systems

b4. Decline in the Value of the
    Products
b5. The Small Trickle of
    Information-Exchange with
    the Sales Department
b6. The Inflexibility of Old
    Systems Continuing

Figure 25 : Mr. Kinouchi's Negative and Positive In-En-Kahoh

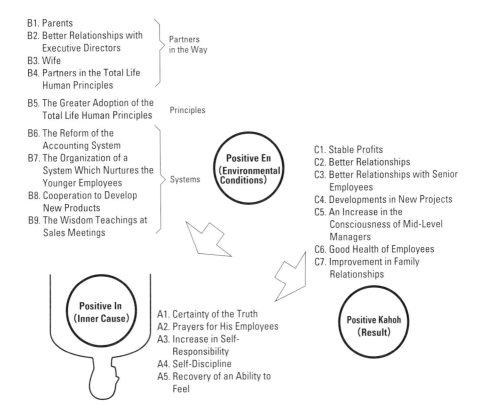

B1. Parents
B2. Better Relationships with
    Executive Directors
B3. Wife
B4. Partners in the Total Life
    Human Principles

Partners
in the Way

B5. The Greater Adoption of the
    Total Life Human Principles

Principles

B6. The Reform of the
    Accounting System
B7. The Organization of a
    System Which Nurtures the
    Younger Employees
B8. Cooperation to Develop
    New Products
B9. The Wisdom Teachings at
    Sales Meetings

Systems

**Positive En
(Environmental
Conditions)**

C1. Stable Profits
C2. Better Relationships
C3. Better Relationships with Senior
    Employees
C4. Developments in New Projects
C5. An Increase in the
    Consciousness of Mid-Level
    Managers
C6. Good Health of Employees
C7. Improvement in Family
    Relationships

**Positive In
(Inner Cause)**

A1. Certainty of the Truth
A2. Prayers for His Employees
A3. Increase in Self-
    Responsibility
A4. Self-Discipline
A5. Recovery of an Ability to
    Feel

**Positive Kahoh
(Result)**

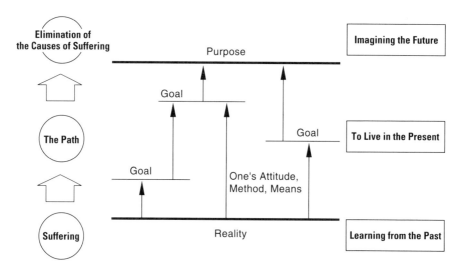

Figure 26 : The Structure of "Wisdom"

to conformity or a lack of innovation and initiative. Mr. Kinouchi, thus, also envisioned a time when his company could grow with fresh and vigorous energy.

These purposes were connected to several specific concerns at Mr. Kinouchi's company: 1) bettering his relationship with executive directors, 2) a more efficient distribution center, and 3) improving profits.

The In-En-Kahoh of Negative Realities 1

In the beginning, these concerns lay within a number of negative realities. In the case of his relationships with his executive directors, we can see how the inner cause (**In**) of his poor relationships lay within himself, for more specifically his "Dependent and Opportunistic Relationships" (a2). This pattern was derived from the **Pleasure-Lethargy** orientation that caused his constant worry about how other people viewed him. Mr. Kinouchi was able to see this pattern in himself after a prolonged period of using the **Reflections and Insight Sheet**. For example, within his mind (inner cause, **In**), he viewed one of his executive directors as "giving a bad impression to our suppliers. I can't help wondering how others view our company." (37) and "It gets hard to make things go smoothly if I don't share the same opinion as Executive Director 'A'." (79). This inner cause was combined with the environmental conditions (**En**, b2) that "When Executive Director 'A' is in a bad mood, it is very apparent. The atmosphere at the company as a whole becomes sour." (04) or "Mid-level managers have been complaining of the lack of access to the executive members of the company." (35). Thus, when these inner cause (**In**) and environmental conditions (**En**) came together, they produced the result (**Kahoh**, c4 "Lack of Ability among Mid-Level Managers"). Because of Mr. Kinouchi's internal attitude, the managers were unable to fully exert their potential, thus leading to this negative result.

The In-En-Kahoh of Negative Realities 2

The second concern at the company, the inefficiency of the distribution center, also can be analyzed in terms of **In-En-Kahoh** (inner cause, environmental conditions, and result). In this case, the **In** [inner cause, a3 "Putting Distance between Himself and Others," especially "Since I haven't been able to visit the distribution center much this past year,

I've left everything up to Department Executive 'B'." (47)], served as the negligent attitude that caused this problem. This was combined with the **En** (environmental conditions), b5 "The Small Trickle of Information-Exchange with the Sales Department" in which he notes "Having put an emphasis on accounting and finances recently, I have been drawn away from the realities of sales." (12) and "I haven't been able to visit the distribution center very often." (40). These conditions functioned as a type of system that emerged at some time or another in which not going to the distribution center became part of a routinized system at the company. Thus this systematic condition at the company was combined with his internal attitude to create the result (c7 "Disorganization at the Distribution Center").

The In-En-Kahohof Negative Realities 3

Finally, if we look at the third major concern at his company, improving profits, we can find a similar process of negative-reality formation. Although he hoped to improve the company's fortunes, a negative orientation was already at work within his mind and in the conditions at the firm. The **In** (inner cause) included, for example, a4 "Conformity without Taking Risks": "Think I've gotten somewhere after a period of study." (41); "Overwhelmed by the schedule, I sometimes give up." (60); and "Now that father is better, I feel that I don't need to make further efforts." (80). This orientation of caution and conformity came about because, although he was concerned that his 200-year-old company did not go under, he didn't see the need for improvement and innovation. This attitude thus led to the **En** (environmental conditions) at the company in which there was a "Decline in the Value of the Products" (b4). There was therefore no incentive to create new and better products as long as existing products were doing decently.

Thus it is not surprising that the following result emerged (c1 "Fragile Profits"): "Sales have been stagnant for three consecutive years." (01); "Good client procurement in the Kanto region, which had come from the efforts of 20 years, has steeply declined in the last three years." (07); "Our new products haven't been catching fire." (16); and "There has been a loss in demand from construction-related industries." (21).

In all three cases of concerns at the company, the function of inner cause and environmental conditions combining to create a negative result was very clear. The **downward spiral** toward negativity only became worse over time, causing further negative realities including (a6, 7, 8—"Pressure Felt from a Lack of Profits," "Giving Up Trying to Change Reality," and "Loneliness and Uncertainty").

But as can be seen from the Charts and Figures related to Mr. Kinouchi, he underwent a process of study based on the Total Life Human Principles, which form the basic teachings of the Grand Challenge. This led to the clear process of turning the negative reality into a positive one at work, at home, and in life in general.

The In-En-Kahoh of Positive Realities 1

This transformation began, first and foremost, as a shift in his mind (**In**) wherein he started to gain confidence in the teachings of the Total Life Human Principles. This appears in the Figure as "Certainty of the Truth" (A1) and especially the entry "Began thinking that I want to be an exemplar of the Total Life Human Principles even though I don't amount to much." (25). With this confidence at the base of his convictions, his attitude in general began to change. Most striking was his "Increase in Self-Responsibility" (A3) and "Self-Discipline" (A4). For example, although Executive Director "A" had been the person with whom Mr. Kinouchi had the least intimacy in the past, as he developed self-confidence and self-discipline, he began to see the positive potential in Executive Director "A." When, at one particularly difficult point in their relationship, "A" asked Mr. Kinouchi for permission to resign from the company, somehow Mr. Kinouchi was able to relate these positive aspects to the man. Not only did he prevent "A" from resigning, he propelled a shift in "A"'s own mind. His earlier mindset would probably have caused a vastly different result, but with his own mind's positive and changed outlook not only did he prevent a negative reality from occurring, but he helped to create a positive one for both himself and Executive Director "A."

These transformations thus resulted in shifts in those around him, so that with more positive environmental conditions (**En**), such as "Better Relationships with Executive Directors" (B2), a more positive result (**Kahoh**) was also created, "An Increase in the Consciousness of Mid-Level Managers" (C5). With Mr. Kinouchi having changed so much and with his clear concern and encouragement (especially to develop a new reality based on the Grand Challenge by the year 2001), his employees have also been moved to change with him.

The In-En-Kahoh of Positive Realities 2

His concern for his employees became particularly apparent in that he could not but pray for his employees' well-being [A2. Prayers for His Employees : "When employees are in the midst of an important phase in their lives, I try to respond appropriately." (13); "Am happy when my employees do good work." (28); and "I have started to dedicate myself to the Total Life Human Principles and to pray for each employee." (52)]. Though he had earlier felt a distance between himself and his employees in a hierarchical structure, he began to feel closer to them, praying for their well-being as he realized that despite the difference in function at the company, everyone was equally a human being. With such a new mindset (**In**), the following environmental conditions (**En**) emerged [B5. The Greater Adoption of the Total Life Human Principles: "The female employees have emphasized friendliness." (15); "Since 1996, the theme 'A Community Bound Together' has been adopted by the employees with the goal of achieving it in the year 2001." (40); "For ten years, our company has maintained a New Year's resolution presentation by the employees for the upcoming year's goals." (42) and "Company employees as a whole have been guided by a yearly theme chosen by the president based on the Total Life Human Principles." (51)].

These new principles that began to guide his company produced clearly-identifiable positive results (**Kahoh**). They included: C2. Better Relationships ["Members of the company have been developing solid relationships with each other." (02); "The female employees have become more energetic and participatory in company-sponsored events." (05); "Several male employees, who up till three years ago didn't participate in company-sponsored events, have all begun to." (06); "The three new employees are all out-going and promising." (33); "Manager 'E''s face has started to cheer up as he has begun looking after those under his supervision more." (83)] as well as C3. Better Relationships with Senior Employees ["In the past three years, although five employees have retired, they have stayed on as directors or part-time employees." (03); "Getting over past disagreements, I managed to develop a friendship with the former Executive Director." (04); "Though the oldest employee of the company, 'F,' has retired, he has continued in good spirits as a part-time employee at the store." (43/2): "Though 'G' has retired from the agro-forestry machine products department, he has continued to help out with the sales as a part-time employee." (44)].

The In-En-Kahoh of Positive Realities 3

These shifts in **In** (inner cause) and **En** (environmental conditions) also made systemic transformations within the company. For example, the company exerted new efforts to promote innovation and new products [B8 "Cooperation to Develop New Products": "Tree planting has been born as a new activity at the company through the joint efforts of the president and the employees." (34) and "Under the supervision of Department Executive 'B,' the retail and facility installation business have increased to the level of the wholesale business of the company." (41)]. Systemic changes like this over time produced positive results (**Kahoh**) not just in particular areas, but throughout the company as a whole [C4 "Developments in New Projects": "The net to prevent wildlife destruction, developed by the agro-forestry machine products department, has recently been adopted at the local forest services department." (37); "The tree planting project, which has not been a profitable division, completed a major project in Shiga Prefecture this past spring." (84); and "Managers 'D' and 'E' have increased their per-unit sales." (85)].

Mr. Kinouchi, in earlier times, could not possibly have imagined that such a workplace, in which young and old employees could work together energetically and with a common purpose, was possible. These positive results (**Kahoh**) could not have come about, however, without a shift in inner cause and environmental conditions (**In** and **En**). Without the president transforming his mind, the environmental conditions (both partners in the Way around him, principles that governed the company, and the system as a whole) could not have shifted. It was the combination of the president's internal changes and the shifts in the external conditions which ultimately brought forth the positive results (**Kahoh**). This is the power of the **Grand Challenge**.

In the present period when many companies are struggling in the midst of a recession in Japan, Mr. Kinouchi's company produced remarkable results. This transformation of his company is clearly a manifestation of his original wish to build a "community bound together." How about his other wish to build a "vibrant, profitable company"?

Three Steps to Building a Vibrant Company

The first step to turning a company around and making it vibrant requires us to ask ourselves "why" and "for what reason" we want to undertake such a task, in other words, an investigation of our intentions. Intentions are important because if the intention to build a vibrant, profitable company is based on the **false self**, then the purpose would simply be for making money and self-gain. This **false self** thus turns the **six forces** into the **six negative conditions**. However, as we have seen throughout this book, such intentions always turn negative and will lead to the eventual decline of a company (based on **the law of disintegration** and **the law of uncontrollability**).

In contrast, our intention must be to draw out the best in people, to fulfill the potential of each employee, through this undertaking. If this is our true intention and wish from the deepest part of our souls, then we will gain the forces from the universe to confront **the law of disintegration** and **the law of uncontrollability**. It will polish our souls and develop the courage and leadership necessary for this task, then we will resonate with the universe.

The reason this intention is so important is because how we position our internal mind (inner cause–**In**) determines whether the **six forces** of the universe go positive or negative (result–**Kahoh**). The human mind ("emptiness" or mind) is what creates the world (form). We humans have yet to recognize just how much our inner disposition creates the world around us. The latent powers of our minds are truly amazing.

The second step in creating a vibrant company, after we have confirmed that our intentions are correct, is to set goals because this is what stops the **downward spiral** and turns us toward a positive reality. If our purpose is to get to the other shore (of liberation) from this bank (of suffering), goals are like the islands that serve as guideposts on the journey. But goals should not be set by fanciful imaginations or by whim or instinct, but rather, goals must be settled on through careful investigation of the positive and negative aspects of **In-En-Kahoh**. The more we look into what creates positive and negative inner cause-environmental conditions-result, for example looking within ourselves with the **Reflections and Insight Sheet**, the easier it will be to set goals.

If the purpose of the undertaking is to create a vibrant and profitable company, for instance, then the goals along the way must be set. In the case of Mr. Kinouchi, who had a personality orientation toward **Pleasure-Lethargy** and **Pain-Lethargy**, he had to set the following set of goals:

1] High Productivity (**In**)—Because of his personality type, he had an orientation to whittle away time. To engage in quality work at a high level of productivity, therefore, was a major goal.

2] Being More Receptive toward Others (**In**)—Mr. Kinouchi also had a personality pattern in which he engaged in shallow and opportunistic relationships. He was able to become more open and receptive toward others by thinking about what the employees were worried and cared about. He encouraged such care for others and the bringing out of each other's potential not only on an individual level, but at the level of each division as well as the company as a whole.

3] Further Studies (**In**)—Though it was easy for Mr. Kinouchi and others not to worry about limits of their knowledge, it became increasingly important for everyone at the firm to challenge themselves to learn more about every aspect of their business.

4] Starting a "Wisdom" Team (**En**)—One of the problems with his company was that because of its lengthy history of 200 years, certain ideas and patterns had entrenched themselves into the entire system of how the company was run. Trying to come out with new "conditions" or systems at the firm required a new approach. One such project was the establishment of a "wisdom" team that could study and solve issues in divisions within the company that were stagnant or not doing very well. This working team, which could also include even the younger employees, would analyze the issues by examining various feedback on what ought to have been done.

5] Starting a Sales Division Research Group (**En**)—Mr. Kinouchi in his analysis of the company often referred to the problems within the sales division. By setting up a research group within the division, both young and more senior employees could discuss sales techniques and philosophies so that all of them could better improve their approach.

These five goals were set up at Mr. Kinouchi's firm as guideposts to help turn around the company from a stagnant to a vibrant one, from a negative to a positive reality. These goals (as islands along the way) required a concrete method to arrive there. It was therefore necessary to engage in the third step of the process, that of setting up a concrete "action program." For example, in terms of the productivity issue, one way to set up a practical "action program" is to first clarify what needs to get done on any particular day. If the tasks are set out clearly, it would be possible to record just how much or how little of those tasks are actually accomplished. Or in terms of the necessity to increase receptivity toward others, one concrete action could be to set up a large blackboard with information about each division's issues, concerns, and potentials in a place that could be easily viewed by the president. More detailed information could be made available to the president through reports filed by individuals or teams. Further, when employees come up with good ideas, they must not only be clearly recognized, but a concrete set of actions to implement them must be set in motion.

It is thus through the examination of one's intentions and clearly marking out the issues, the setting up of goals, and the setting in motion of a concrete action program that enable the negative reality to turn toward the positive.

The Path to the New Millennium : The Actualization of Turning the Six Forces into a Positive Reality

"Without inner cause and environmental conditions (**In-En**), there are no results (**Kahoh**)." This principle of **In-En-Kahoh** has been at the base of our discussion of the **Grand Challenge**, characterized by the practices **to look within ourselves** and **to connect our inner selves and the outer world**. We saw in the above example of Mr. Kinouchi's company just how, by understanding the principle, he was able to shift the negative energies into a positive reality.

At first, reality appears before us as chaos with both negative and positive energies swirling around us. But by examining this **chaos** closely, we have also learned how it is possible to distinguish and delineate the negative from the positive. Through this investigation, we have studied how by transforming our inner mindset (**In**) and environmental conditions (**En**), it is possible to put a stop to the negative reality and turn it into a positive one (a new result as it were, the **Kahoh**). This process of turning reality into a positive one is further marked by the necessity of putting up "goals" as guideposts along the way of actualizing a new reality.

In the chaotic reality that we face, there are hidden structures. It is possible to shed light upon those structures through the law of **In-En-Kahoh** and the principle of the **Grand Challenge** and it is possible to resonate with the forces of the universe to create a positive reality. To turn the **six forces** of the universe toward the positive in this way is precisely what the new millennium calls us to undertake as the **Grand Challenge**.

EPILOGUE

Toward a Vivid Transformation

Although the phrases **to look within ourselves** and **to connect our inner selves and the outer world** may have seemed like simple enough concepts for you at the beginning of this book, hopefully this impression has changed dramatically in the course of reading this volume. If it were possible, I would want to meet each one of you face to face to learn how the book impacted you. How you have come to understand these concepts will, without doubt, make a tremendous impact on your life from here on out. The deep and nuanced step-by-step aspects of the teachings of the Grand Challenge is your challenge. It requires you to study and walk a path, one that becomes richer and more fulfilling, the more one realizes the simplicity of its principles. It is my heartfelt wish that you succeed along this journey.

This work, *The Grand Challenge*, is part of a trilogy of books written recently (the other two are *The Principle of Hope* and *Discovery*). While each book stands alone, they can also be read side by side as a set because together they explain a new basic philosophy (the discovery of a thick veil that covers the human soul, *Discovery*), a new identification of one's life mission (the idea that "hope" represents the fundamental structure of the universe and the human mission in life, *The Principle of Hope*), and a new vision of human-universe resonance (on how to create a new reality in resonance with the universe, *The Grand Challenge*). This trilogy has been six years in the making and it is beyond words for me to describe how profound the process of putting the three visions together has been.

These writings were the result of many people studying and participating in these teachings with me. With this final book of the trilogy, it is my sincere hope that if even one more human soul comes into contact with these teachings, we will be able to enact a tremendous and vivid transformation of our world as we create the new millennium. This invitation to engage in the creation of this new age and new world, a hope that has resided in the depths of each person's soul, is my Grand Challenge to you.